Hook-ups & Hang-overs

A Journal

How
drunk
was I?
And who
are you?

CHRONICLE BOOKS

SAN FRANCISCO

ISBN 978-1-4521-0289-4

Manufactured in China
Design by Michael Morris

10 9 8 7 6 5 4 3

Chronicle Books
680 Second Street
San Francisco, CA 94107
www.chroniclebooks.com

It's a glorious new day.

The sun is shining, the birds are singing, and the water is overflowing down the hall. Wait. Where am I? Who is *that*? WTF?

Relax. It's happened to all of us: You wake up in a kiddie pool wearing a party hat and roller skates next to a complete stranger. You've got a pounding hangover and no memory of how you got there.

By afternoon, hopefully the hangover will have worn off, but the lingering questions will remain. Where's my phone? How come I'm wearing only one shoe? Is that a *hickey*? How did I get a hickey on my *ankle*? Who did I make out with? Did I throw up on them? Is any of this on the Web?

Fortunately, you no longer have to wonder. *Hookups & Hangovers* will help you reconstruct the night before and fill in the blurry blanks. It will remind you where you might have left your coat, who you need to make apology calls to, and which bar you can never show your face in again. It will help you avoid future disasters, allowing you to track which drinks make for a fun night, and which ones inevitably lead to ill-advised behavior.

Think of it as a handy reference guide you can take with you when you head out for that night of self-induced amnesia. When you're drinking, you might forget that Alex is a total douche unworthy of a hookup; that you do *not* look cool doing the robot; that "My Heart Will Go On" is not a good karaoke choice for you; and that even though it sounds good at the time, eating a super burrito at 2 A.M. isn't a great idea. Not to worry. Your trusty journal is right there, like a loyal friend, to remind you of what you can't always remember yourself.

With a few party tips and hangover cures to ease your suffering, *Hookups & Hangovers* is here to help you learn from your mistakes, so that you can go out and make a whole bunch more of them. There are strangers to be smooched and drinks to be drunk, so let's get going. The cab is waiting outside, and that backseat is not going to throw up on itself.

Cheers!

The morning after brings so many questions: Who, what, when, where, and why, oh why? How come it feels like there's a jackhammer crew in my head, and what will make it stop? Here are a few answers:

What Causes a Hangover?

Hangovers can be caused by many things: a recent breakup, a bad day at work, boredom, or two-for-one night at Shooters' Fun Time Alley. Whatever prompted it, the simple answer is you drank way too much, which caused your body to do a whole host of things that are making you feel rotten right now. Alcohol is a diuretic, which makes you have to pee and leaves you totally dehydrated. This is what's causing your pounding headache. You're nauseous because of alcohol's effects on your stomach. One drink too many can irritate and inflame that stomach lining. Finally, your liver is tied up trying to process all that tequila, leaving it too busy to do its normal job of breaking down glucose. This results in low blood sugar, which is making you feel grumpy and lousy all around. Good times!

What Cures a Hangover?

 First of all, no one needs six margaritas. For those of us who do need three, don't drink them on an empty stomach and remember that water is a drinker's best friend. While you're out on the town, try to drink one glass of water for every alcoholic beverage. Drink more water before you go to bed, and when you get up, hit the H_2O again. Even better: Try coconut water. It contains the same electrolytes found in human blood—calcium, phosphorus, potassium, magnesium, and sodium—while sports drinks have only two.

Vitamins—especially B and C—can help your body get back to a normal functioning state. Resting and sleeping always work wonders. If you can get out of bed, try going for a walk and working those toxins out of your system. Some people swear by the curative properties of a greasy breakfast. Others skip right to the Bloody Mary for some hair of the dog. To be fair, this is probably just delaying the hangover rather than curing it, but at least the celery and tomato juice are healthy, kind of like a liquid salad. In the end, do whatever you need to do and remember that tomorrow you'll feel better than today.

HANGOVERS

Hangover rating ☐ Still drunk

☐ A glass of water and good to go
☐ Greasy breakfast, please
☐ Throbbing headache
☐ Feeling pretty crappy

☐ Everything is spinning
☐ Afterparty in the bathroom
☐ Can't move / Never getting out of bed
☐ **Never** drinking again

Where did I wake up?

_____

☐ Alone ☐ With _____ ☐ WTF ☐ Walk of shame

The last thing I remember:

_____
_____

Where I went last night / details:

_____
_____

I drank:

_____
_____
_____

I got:

☐ Buzzed   ☐ Wasted
☐ Tipsy   ☐ Sh*t-faced
☐ Drunk   ☐ Annihilated

I lost:

☐ Keys ☐ Phone ☐ Wallet ☐ Dignity ☐ Other _____

I can't believe I:

☐ Puked—How many times / where / on whom? _____
☐ Drunk dialed / texted / emailed _____
☐ Other awesomeness _____

HOOKUPS

Who: _____ ☐ No clue

Where: _____

Looks: ☆ ☆ ☆ ☆ ☆   ☐ Butt ugly   ☐ Doesn't matter
                           ☐ Super hot   ☐ Beer goggles

Personality: ☆ ☆ ☆ ☆ ☆   ☐ Zero   ☐ Soul mate
                               ☐ Just okay   ☐ Who cares

Details: **I think he/she looked like:**

_____

_____

_____

_____

_____

_____

How hot did it get?

☐ ZZZ   ☐ G   ☐ PG   ☐ PG-13   ☐ R   ☐ NC-17   ☐ X   ☐ XXX

Next steps?

☐ Avoid   ☐ Stalk   ☐ Go to church   ☐ Get tested   ☐ Hit that again

Note to self:

_____

_____

Remember to drink a glass of water for every glass of alcohol and drink
more water before you go to bed. Coconut water is also super hydrating,
as it contains essential electrolytes.

HANGOVERS

Hangover rating ☐ Still drunk

☐ A glass of water and good to go
☐ Greasy breakfast, please
☐ Throbbing headache
☐ Feeling pretty crappy

☐ Everything is spinning
☐ Afterparty in the bathroom
☐ Can't move / Never getting out of bed
☐ **Never** drinking again

Where did I wake up?

_____

☐ Alone ☐ With _____ ☐ WTF ☐ Walk of shame

The last thing I remember:

_____

_____

Where I went last night / details:

_____

_____

I drank:

_____

_____

_____

I got:

☐ Buzzed ☐ Wasted
☐ Tipsy ☐ Sh*t-faced
☐ Drunk ☐ Annihilated

I lost:

☐ Keys ☐ Phone ☐ Wallet ☐ Dignity ☐ Other _____

I can't believe I:

☐ Puked—How many times / where / on whom? _____
☐ Drunk dialed / texted / emailed _____
☐ Other awesomeness _____

_____

HOOKUPS

Who: _____ ☐ No clue

Where: _____

Looks: ☆ ☆ ☆ ☆ ☆   ☐ Butt ugly   ☐ Doesn't matter
                          ☐ Super hot   ☐ Beer goggles

Personality: ☆ ☆ ☆ ☆ ☆   ☐ Zero   ☐ Soul mate
                               ☐ Just okay   ☐ Who cares

Details:

_____

_____

_____

_____

_____

_____

I think he/she looked like:

SKETCH HERE

How hot did it get?

☐ ZZZ   ☐ G   ☐ PG   ☐ PG-13   ☐ R   ☐ NC-17   ☐ X   ☐ XXX

Next steps?

☐ Avoid   ☐ Stalk   ☐ Go to church   ☐ Get tested   ☐ Hit that again

Note to self:

_____

_____

Consider swapping your bourbon for vodka. Darker liquors contain more congeners, by-products of alcohol fermentation, which are believed to make hangovers worse.

HANGOVERS

Hangover rating ☐ Still drunk

☐ A glass of water and good to go
☐ Greasy breakfast, please
☐ Throbbing headache
☐ Feeling pretty crappy

☐ Everything is spinning
☐ Afterparty in the bathroom
☐ Can't move / Never getting out of bed
☐ **Never** drinking again

Where did I wake up?

_____

☐ Alone ☐ With _____ ☐ WTF ☐ Walk of shame

The last thing I remember:

_____
_____

Where I went last night / details:

_____
_____

I drank:

_____

_____

_____

I got:

☐ Buzzed ☐ Wasted
☐ Tipsy ☐ Sh*t-faced
☐ Drunk ☐ Annihilated

I lost:

☐ Keys ☐ Phone ☐ Wallet ☐ Dignity ☐ Other _____

I can't believe I:

☐ Puked—How many times / where / on whom? _____
☐ Drunk dialed / texted / emailed _____
☐ Other awesomeness _____

HOOKUPS

Who: _____ ☐ No clue

Where: _____

Looks: ☆ ☆ ☆ ☆ ☆ ☐ Butt ugly   ☐ Doesn't matter
 ☐ Super hot   ☐ Beer goggles

Personality: ☆ ☆ ☆ ☆ ☆ ☐ Zero   ☐ Soul mate
 ☐ Just okay   ☐ Who cares

Details: **I think he/she looked like:**

_____

_____

_____

_____

_____

_____

How hot did it get?

☐ ZZZ ☐ G ☐ PG ☐ PG-13 ☐ R ☐ NC-17 ☐ X ☐ XXX

Next steps?

☐ Avoid ☐ Stalk ☐ Go to church ☐ Get tested ☐ Hit that again

Note to self:

_____

_____

After a night of fun times, eat something before crawling into bed.
Bananas are a great choice—they contain potassium, which alcohol
consumption depletes from your body, and B_6, which is claimed to
be a great hangover killer.

HANGOVERS

DATE

Hangover rating ☐ Still drunk

☐ A glass of water and good to go
☐ Greasy breakfast, please
☐ Throbbing headache
☐ Feeling pretty crappy

☐ Everything is spinning
☐ Afterparty in the bathroom
☐ Can't move / Never getting out of bed
☐ **Never** drinking again

Where did I wake up?

_____

☐ Alone ☐ With _____ ☐ WTF ☐ Walk of shame

The last thing I remember:

_____
_____

Where I went last night / details:

_____
_____

I drank:

_____
_____
_____

I got:

☐ Buzzed ☐ Wasted
☐ Tipsy ☐ Sh*t-faced
☐ Drunk ☐ Annihilated

I lost:

☐ Keys ☐ Phone ☐ Wallet ☐ Dignity ☐ Other _____

I can't believe I:

☐ Puked—How many times / where / on whom? _____
☐ Drunk dialed / texted / emailed _____
☐ Other awesomeness _____

HOOKUPS

Who: _____ ☐ No clue

Where: _____

Looks: ☆ ☆ ☆ ☆ ☆   ☐ Butt ugly   ☐ Doesn't matter
                                      ☐ Super hot   ☐ Beer goggles

Personality: ☆ ☆ ☆ ☆ ☆   ☐ Zero   ☐ Soul mate
                                        ☐ Just okay   ☐ Who cares

Details: **I think he/she looked like:**

_____

_____

_____

_____

_____

_____

How hot did it get?

☐ ZZZ   ☐ G   ☐ PG   ☐ PG-13   ☐ R   ☐ NC-17   ☐ X   ☐ XXX

Next steps?

☐ Avoid   ☐ Stalk   ☐ Go to church   ☐ Get tested   ☐ Hit that again

Note to self:

_____

_____

> If you have friends who think it's funny to write on the passed-out person's forehead, remember to look in a mirror before you leave the house today.

HANGOVERS

DATE

Hangover rating ☐ Still drunk

☐ A glass of water and good to go
☐ Greasy breakfast, please
☐ Throbbing headache
☐ Feeling pretty crappy

☐ Everything is spinning
☐ Afterparty in the bathroom
☐ Can't move / Never getting out of bed
☐ **Never** drinking again

Where did I wake up?

_____

☐ Alone ☐ With _____ ☐ WTF ☐ Walk of shame

The last thing I remember:

_____

_____

Where I went last night / details:

_____

_____

I drank:

_____

_____

_____

I got:

☐ Buzzed ☐ Wasted
☐ Tipsy ☐ Sh*t-faced
☐ Drunk ☐ Annihilated

I lost:

☐ Keys ☐ Phone ☐ Wallet ☐ Dignity ☐ Other _____

I can't believe I:

☐ Puked—How many times / where / on whom? _____
☐ Drunk dialed / texted / emailed _____
☐ Other awesomeness _____

HOOKUPS

Who: _____ ☐ No clue

Where: _____

Looks: ☆ ☆ ☆ ☆ ☆   ☐ Butt ugly   ☐ Doesn't matter
                                      ☐ Super hot   ☐ Beer goggles

Personality: ☆ ☆ ☆ ☆ ☆   ☐ Zero   ☐ Soul mate
                                      ☐ Just okay   ☐ Who cares

Details: **I think he/she looked like:**

_____

_____

_____

_____

_____

_____

How hot did it get?

☐ ZZZ   ☐ G   ☐ PG   ☐ PG-13   ☐ R   ☐ NC-17   ☐ X   ☐ XXX

Next steps?

☐ Avoid   ☐ Stalk   ☐ Go to church   ☐ Get tested   ☐ Hit that again

Note to self:

_____

_____

> You're not imagining it: Your hangovers really are getting worse. That's because as you age, you produce less alcohol dehydrogenase, the enzyme that breaks down alcohol.

HANGOVERS

Hangover rating ☐ Still drunk

☐ A glass of water and good to go   ☐ Everything is spinning
☐ Greasy breakfast, please   ☐ Afterparty in the bathroom
☐ Throbbing headache   ☐ Can't move / Never getting out of bed
☐ Feeling pretty crappy   ☐ **Never** drinking again

Where did I wake up?

_____

☐ Alone ☐ With _____ ☐ WTF ☐ Walk of shame

The last thing I remember:

_____
_____

Where I went last night / details:

_____
_____

I drank:

_____

_____

_____

I got:

☐ Buzzed   ☐ Wasted
☐ Tipsy   ☐ Sh*t-faced
☐ Drunk   ☐ Annihilated

I lost:

☐ Keys ☐ Phone ☐ Wallet ☐ Dignity ☐ Other _____

I can't believe I:

☐ Puked—How many times / where / on whom? _____
☐ Drunk dialed / texted / emailed _____
☐ Other awesomeness _____

HOOKUPS

Who: _____ ☐ No clue

Where: _____

Looks: ☆ ☆ ☆ ☆ ☆   ☐ Butt ugly   ☐ Doesn't matter
                            ☐ Super hot   ☐ Beer goggles

Personality: ☆ ☆ ☆ ☆ ☆   ☐ Zero   ☐ Soul mate
                                  ☐ Just okay   ☐ Who cares

Details: **I think he/she looked like:**

_____

_____

_____

_____

_____

_____

How hot did it get?

☐ ZZZ   ☐ G   ☐ PG   ☐ PG-13   ☐ R   ☐ NC-17   ☐ X   ☐ XXX

Next steps?

☐ Avoid   ☐ Stalk   ☐ Go to church   ☐ Get tested   ☐ Hit that again

Note to self:

_____

_____

> Hey, drunky, put down the phone. Drunk dialing or texting always results in embarrassing apology dialing the next day.

HANGOVERS

DATE

Hangover rating ☐ Still drunk

☐ A glass of water and good to go
☐ Greasy breakfast, please
☐ Throbbing headache
☐ Feeling pretty crappy

☐ Everything is spinning
☐ Afterparty in the bathroom
☐ Can't move / Never getting out of bed
☐ **Never** drinking again

Where did I wake up?

_____

☐ Alone ☐ With _____ ☐ WTF ☐ Walk of shame

The last thing I remember:

_____

_____

Where I went last night / details:

_____

_____

I drank:

_____

_____

_____

I got:

☐ Buzzed ☐ Wasted
☐ Tipsy ☐ Sh*t-faced
☐ Drunk ☐ Annihilated

I lost:

☐ Keys ☐ Phone ☐ Wallet ☐ Dignity ☐ Other _____

I can't believe I:

☐ Puked—How many times / where / on whom? _____
☐ Drunk dialed / texted / emailed _____
☐ Other awesomeness _____

HOOKUPS

Who: _____ ☐ No clue

Where: _____

Looks: ☆ ☆ ☆ ☆ ☆   ☐ Butt ugly   ☐ Doesn't matter
                              ☐ Super hot   ☐ Beer goggles

Personality: ☆ ☆ ☆ ☆ ☆   ☐ Zero   ☐ Soul mate
                                   ☐ Just okay   ☐ Who cares

Details: **I think he/she looked like:**

_____

_____

_____

_____

_____

_____

How hot did it get?

☐ ZZZ   ☐ G   ☐ PG   ☐ PG-13   ☐ R   ☐ NC-17   ☐ X   ☐ XXX

Next steps?

☐ Avoid   ☐ Stalk   ☐ Go to church   ☐ Get tested   ☐ Hit that again

Note to self:

_____

_____

Sunglasses are essential for concealing bleary, hungover eyes and making
the walk of shame a little less shameful.

HANGOVERS

DATE

Hangover rating ☐ Still drunk

☐ A glass of water and good to go
☐ Greasy breakfast, please
☐ Throbbing headache
☐ Feeling pretty crappy

☐ Everything is spinning
☐ Afterparty in the bathroom
☐ Can't move / Never getting out of bed
☐ **Never** drinking again

Where did I wake up?

_____

☐ Alone ☐ With _____ ☐ WTF ☐ Walk of shame

The last thing I remember:

_____
_____

Where I went last night / details:

_____
_____

I drank:

_____
_____
_____

I got:

☐ Buzzed ☐ Wasted
☐ Tipsy ☐ Sh*t-faced
☐ Drunk ☐ Annihilated

I lost:

☐ Keys ☐ Phone ☐ Wallet ☐ Dignity ☐ Other _____

I can't believe I:

☐ Puked—How many times / where / on whom? _____
☐ Drunk dialed / texted / emailed _____
☐ Other awesomeness _____

HOOKUPS

Who: _____ ☐ No clue

Where: _____

Looks: ☆ ☆ ☆ ☆ ☆   ☐ Butt ugly   ☐ Doesn't matter
                                        ☐ Super hot   ☐ Beer goggles

Personality: ☆ ☆ ☆ ☆ ☆   ☐ Zero   ☐ Soul mate
                                              ☐ Just okay   ☐ Who cares

Details: **I think he/she looked like:**

_____

_____

_____

_____

_____

How hot did it get?

☐ ZZZ   ☐ G   ☐ PG   ☐ PG-13   ☐ R   ☐ NC-17   ☐ X   ☐ XXX

Next steps?

☐ Avoid   ☐ Stalk   ☐ Go to church   ☐ Get tested   ☐ Hit that again

Note to self:

_____

_____

> It's been said that drinking a glass of milk or a spoonful of olive oil before consuming alcohol can help prevent a hangover. The milk and oil coat the stomach lining and slow down the absorption of alcohol.

HANGOVERS

DATE

Hangover rating ☐ Still drunk

☐ A glass of water and good to go
☐ Greasy breakfast, please
☐ Throbbing headache
☐ Feeling pretty crappy

☐ Everything is spinning
☐ Afterparty in the bathroom
☐ Can't move / Never getting out of bed
☐ **Never** drinking again

Where did I wake up?

_____

☐ Alone ☐ With _____ ☐ WTF ☐ Walk of shame

The last thing I remember:

_____
_____

Where I went last night / details:

_____
_____

I drank:

_____
_____
_____

I got:

☐ Buzzed ☐ Wasted
☐ Tipsy ☐ Sh*t-faced
☐ Drunk ☐ Annihilated

I lost:

☐ Keys ☐ Phone ☐ Wallet ☐ Dignity ☐ Other _____

I can't believe I:

☐ Puked—How many times / where / on whom? _____
☐ Drunk dialed / texted / emailed _____
☐ Other awesomeness _____

HOOKUPS

Who: _____ ☐ No clue

Where: _____

Looks: ☆ ☆ ☆ ☆ ☆   ☐ Butt ugly   ☐ Doesn't matter
                         ☐ Super hot   ☐ Beer goggles

Personality: ☆ ☆ ☆ ☆ ☆   ☐ Zero   ☐ Soul mate
                               ☐ Just okay   ☐ Who cares

Details:

_____

_____

_____

_____

_____

_____

I think he/she looked like:

How hot did it get?

☐ ZZZ ☐ G ☐ PG ☐ PG-13 ☐ R ☐ NC-17 ☐ X ☐ XXX

Next steps?

☐ Avoid ☐ Stalk ☐ Go to church ☐ Get tested ☐ Hit that again

Note to self:

_____

_____

> Remember to drink a glass of water for every glass of alcohol and drink more water before you go to bed. Coconut water is also super hydrating, as it contains essential electrolytes.

HANGOVERS

Hangover rating ☐ Still drunk

☐ A glass of water and good to go
☐ Greasy breakfast, please
☐ Throbbing headache
☐ Feeling pretty crappy

☐ Everything is spinning
☐ Afterparty in the bathroom
☐ Can't move / Never getting out of bed
☐ **Never** drinking again

Where did I wake up?

_____

☐ Alone ☐ With _____ ☐ WTF ☐ Walk of shame

The last thing I remember:

_____
_____

Where I went last night / details:

_____
_____

I drank:

_____

_____

_____

I got:

☐ Buzzed ☐ Wasted
☐ Tipsy ☐ Sh*t-faced
☐ Drunk ☐ Annihilated

I lost:

☐ Keys ☐ Phone ☐ Wallet ☐ Dignity ☐ Other _____

I can't believe I:

☐ Puked—How many times / where / on whom? _____
☐ Drunk dialed / texted / emailed _____
☐ Other awesomeness _____

HOOKUPS

Who: _____ ☐ No clue

Where: _____

Looks: ☆ ☆ ☆ ☆ ☆   ☐ Butt ugly   ☐ Doesn't matter
                                      ☐ Super hot   ☐ Beer goggles

Personality: ☆ ☆ ☆ ☆ ☆   ☐ Zero   ☐ Soul mate
                                      ☐ Just okay   ☐ Who cares

Details: **I think he/she looked like:**

_____

_____

_____

_____

_____

_____

How hot did it get?

☐ ZZZ   ☐ G   ☐ PG   ☐ PG-13   ☐ R   ☐ NC-17   ☐ X   ☐ XXX

Next steps?

☐ Avoid   ☐ Stalk   ☐ Go to church   ☐ Get tested   ☐ Hit that again

Note to self:

_____

_____

Consider swapping your bourbon for vodka. Darker liquors contain more congeners, by-products of alcohol fermentation, which are believed to make hangovers worse.

HANGOVERS

DATE

Hangover rating   ☐ Still drunk

☐ A glass of water and good to go
☐ Greasy breakfast, please
☐ Throbbing headache
☐ Feeling pretty crappy

☐ Everything is spinning
☐ Afterparty in the bathroom
☐ Can't move / Never getting out of bed
☐ **Never** drinking again

Where did I wake up?

_____

☐ Alone ☐ With _____ ☐ WTF ☐ Walk of shame

The last thing I remember:

_____

_____

Where I went last night / details:

_____

_____

I drank:

_____

_____

_____

I got:

☐ Buzzed   ☐ Wasted
☐ Tipsy   ☐ Sh*t-faced
☐ Drunk   ☐ Annihilated

I lost:

☐ Keys ☐ Phone ☐ Wallet ☐ Dignity ☐ Other _____

I can't believe I:

☐ Puked—How many times / where / on whom? _____
☐ Drunk dialed / texted / emailed _____
☐ Other awesomeness _____

HOOKUPS

Who: _____ ☐ No clue

Where: _____

Looks: ☆ ☆ ☆ ☆ ☆   ☐ Butt ugly   ☐ Doesn't matter
                                   ☐ Super hot   ☐ Beer goggles

Personality: ☆ ☆ ☆ ☆ ☆   ☐ Zero   ☐ Soul mate
                                   ☐ Just okay   ☐ Who cares

Details: **I think he/she looked like:**

_____

_____

_____

_____

_____

_____

SKETCH HERE

How hot did it get?

☐ ZZZ   ☐ G   ☐ PG   ☐ PG-13   ☐ R   ☐ NC-17   ☐ X   ☐ XXX

Next steps?

☐ Avoid   ☐ Stalk   ☐ Go to church   ☐ Get tested   ☐ Hit that again

Note to self:

_____

_____

After a night of fun times, eat something before crawling into bed.
Bananas are a great choice—they contain potassium, which alcohol
consumption depletes from your body, and B_6, which is claimed to
be a great hangover killer.

HANGOVERS

DATE

Hangover rating ☐ Still drunk

☐ A glass of water and good to go
☐ Greasy breakfast, please
☐ Throbbing headache
☐ Feeling pretty crappy

☐ Everything is spinning
☐ Afterparty in the bathroom
☐ Can't move / Never getting out of bed
☐ **Never** drinking again

Where did I wake up?

_____

☐ Alone ☐ With _____ ☐ WTF ☐ Walk of shame

The last thing I remember:

_____

_____

Where I went last night / details:

_____

_____

I drank:

_____

_____

_____

I got:

☐ Buzzed ☐ Wasted
☐ Tipsy ☐ Sh*t-faced
☐ Drunk ☐ Annihilated

I lost:

☐ Keys ☐ Phone ☐ Wallet ☐ Dignity ☐ Other _____

I can't believe I:

☐ Puked—How many times / where / on whom? _____

☐ Drunk dialed / texted / emailed _____

☐ Other awesomeness _____

HOOKUPS

Who: _____ ☐ No clue

Where: _____

Looks: ☆ ☆ ☆ ☆ ☆   ☐ Butt ugly   ☐ Doesn't matter
                                 ☐ Super hot   ☐ Beer goggles

Personality: ☆ ☆ ☆ ☆ ☆   ☐ Zero   ☐ Soul mate
                                          ☐ Just okay   ☐ Who cares

Details: **I think he/she looked like:**

_____

_____

_____

_____

_____

_____

How hot did it get?

☐ ZZZ   ☐ G   ☐ PG   ☐ PG-13   ☐ R   ☐ NC-17   ☐ X   ☐ XXX

Next steps?

☐ Avoid   ☐ Stalk   ☐ Go to church   ☐ Get tested   ☐ Hit that again

Note to self:

_____

_____

> If you have friends who think it's funny to write on the passed-out person's forehead, remember to look in a mirror before you leave the house today.

HANGOVERS

Hangover rating ☐ Still drunk

☐ A glass of water and good to go   ☐ Everything is spinning
☐ Greasy breakfast, please   ☐ Afterparty in the bathroom
☐ Throbbing headache   ☐ Can't move / Never getting out of bed
☐ Feeling pretty crappy   ☐ **Never** drinking again

Where did I wake up?

_____

☐ Alone ☐ With _____ ☐ WTF ☐ Walk of shame

The last thing I remember:

_____
_____

Where I went last night / details:

_____
_____

I drank:

_____

_____

_____

I got:

☐ Buzzed   ☐ Wasted
☐ Tipsy   ☐ Sh*t-faced
☐ Drunk   ☐ Annihilated

I lost:

☐ Keys ☐ Phone ☐ Wallet ☐ Dignity ☐ Other _____

I can't believe I:

☐ Puked—How many times / where / on whom? _____

☐ Drunk dialed / texted / emailed _____

☐ Other awesomeness _____

HOOKUPS

Who: _____ ☐ No clue

Where: _____

Looks: ☆ ☆ ☆ ☆ ☆   ☐ Butt ugly   ☐ Doesn't matter
                          ☐ Super hot   ☐ Beer goggles

Personality: ☆ ☆ ☆ ☆ ☆   ☐ Zero   ☐ Soul mate
                                ☐ Just okay   ☐ Who cares

Details: **I think he/she looked like:**

_____

_____

_____

_____

_____

How hot did it get?

☐ ZZZ ☐ G ☐ PG ☐ PG-13 ☐ R ☐ NC-17 ☐ X ☐ XXX

Next steps?

☐ Avoid ☐ Stalk ☐ Go to church ☐ Get tested ☐ Hit that again

Note to self:

_____

_____

You're not imagining it: Your hangovers really are getting worse. That's
because as you age, you produce less alcohol dehydrogenase, the
enzyme that breaks down alcohol.

HANGOVERS

Hangover rating   ☐ Still drunk

☐ A glass of water and good to go   ☐ Everything is spinning
☐ Greasy breakfast, please   ☐ Afterparty in the bathroom
☐ Throbbing headache   ☐ Can't move / Never getting out of bed
☐ Feeling pretty crappy   ☐ **Never** drinking again

Where did I wake up?

_____

☐ Alone ☐ With _____ ☐ WTF ☐ Walk of shame

The last thing I remember:

_____
_____

Where I went last night / details:

_____
_____

I drank:

_____

_____

_____

I got:

☐ Buzzed   ☐ Wasted
☐ Tipsy   ☐ Sh*t-faced
☐ Drunk   ☐ Annihilated

I lost:

☐ Keys ☐ Phone ☐ Wallet ☐ Dignity ☐ Other _____

I can't believe I:

☐ Puked—How many times / where / on whom? _____
☐ Drunk dialed / texted / emailed _____
☐ Other awesomeness _____

HOOKUPS

Who: _____ ☐ No clue

Where: _____

Looks: ☆ ☆ ☆ ☆ ☆   ☐ Butt ugly   ☐ Doesn't matter
                          ☐ Super hot   ☐ Beer goggles

Personality: ☆ ☆ ☆ ☆ ☆   ☐ Zero   ☐ Soul mate
                              ☐ Just okay   ☐ Who cares

Details: **I think he/she looked like:**

_____

_____

_____

_____

_____

_____

How hot did it get?

☐ ZZZ   ☐ G   ☐ PG   ☐ PG-13   ☐ R   ☐ NC-17   ☐ X   ☐ XXX

Next steps?

☐ Avoid   ☐ Stalk   ☐ Go to church   ☐ Get tested   ☐ Hit that again

Note to self:

_____

_____

Hey, drunky, put down the phone. Drunk dialing or texting always results
in embarrassing apology dialing the next day.

HANGOVERS

DATE

Hangover rating ☐ Still drunk

☐ A glass of water and good to go
☐ Greasy breakfast, please
☐ Throbbing headache
☐ Feeling pretty crappy

☐ Everything is spinning
☐ Afterparty in the bathroom
☐ Can't move / Never getting out of bed
☐ **Never** drinking again

Where did I wake up?

_____

☐ Alone ☐ With _____ ☐ WTF ☐ Walk of shame

The last thing I remember:

_____

_____

Where I went last night / details:

_____

_____

I drank:

_____

_____

_____

I got:

☐ Buzzed ☐ Wasted
☐ Tipsy ☐ Sh*t-faced
☐ Drunk ☐ Annihilated

I lost:

☐ Keys ☐ Phone ☐ Wallet ☐ Dignity ☐ Other _____

I can't believe I:

☐ Puked—How many times / where / on whom? _____
☐ Drunk dialed / texted / emailed _____
☐ Other awesomeness _____

_____

HOOKUPS

Who: _____ ☐ No clue

Where: _____

Looks: ☆ ☆ ☆ ☆ ☆   ☐ Butt ugly   ☐ Doesn't matter
                          ☐ Super hot   ☐ Beer goggles

Personality: ☆ ☆ ☆ ☆ ☆   ☐ Zero   ☐ Soul mate
                              ☐ Just okay   ☐ Who cares

Details: **I think he/she looked like:**

_____

_____

_____

_____

_____

_____

How hot did it get?

☐ ZZZ   ☐ G   ☐ PG   ☐ PG-13   ☐ R   ☐ NC-17   ☐ X   ☐ XXX

Next steps?

☐ Avoid   ☐ Stalk   ☐ Go to church   ☐ Get tested   ☐ Hit that again

Note to self:

_____

_____

Sunglasses are essential for concealing bleary, hungover eyes and making
the walk of shame a little less shameful.

HANGOVERS

DATE

Hangover rating ☐ Still drunk

☐ A glass of water and good to go
☐ Greasy breakfast, please
☐ Throbbing headache
☐ Feeling pretty crappy

☐ Everything is spinning
☐ Afterparty in the bathroom
☐ Can't move / Never getting out of bed
☐ **Never** drinking again

Where did I wake up?

_____

☐ Alone ☐ With _____ ☐ WTF ☐ Walk of shame

The last thing I remember:

_____
_____

Where I went last night / details:

_____
_____

I drank:

_____

_____

_____

I got:

☐ Buzzed ☐ Wasted
☐ Tipsy ☐ Sh*t-faced
☐ Drunk ☐ Annihilated

I lost:

☐ Keys ☐ Phone ☐ Wallet ☐ Dignity ☐ Other _____

I can't believe I:

☐ Puked—How many times / where / on whom? _____

☐ Drunk dialed / texted / emailed _____

☐ Other awesomeness _____

HOOKUPS

Who: _____ ☐ No clue

Where: _____

Looks: ☆ ☆ ☆ ☆ ☆ ☐ Butt ugly   ☐ Doesn't matter
☐ Super hot   ☐ Beer goggles

Personality: ☆ ☆ ☆ ☆ ☆ ☐ Zero   ☐ Soul mate
☐ Just okay   ☐ Who cares

Details: **I think he/she looked like:**

_____

_____

_____

_____

_____

_____

How hot did it get?

☐ ZZZ   ☐ G   ☐ PG   ☐ PG-13   ☐ R   ☐ NC-17   ☐ X   ☐ XXX

Next steps?

☐ Avoid   ☐ Stalk   ☐ Go to church   ☐ Get tested   ☐ Hit that again

Note to self:

_____

_____

It's been said that drinking a glass of milk or a spoonful of olive oil before consuming alcohol can help prevent a hangover. The milk and oil coat the stomach lining and slow down the absorption of alcohol.

HANGOVERS

Hangover rating ☐ Still drunk

☐ A glass of water and good to go
☐ Greasy breakfast, please
☐ Throbbing headache
☐ Feeling pretty crappy

☐ Everything is spinning
☐ Afterparty in the bathroom
☐ Can't move / Never getting out of bed
☐ **Never** drinking again

Where did I wake up?

_____

☐ Alone ☐ With _____ ☐ WTF ☐ Walk of shame

The last thing I remember:

_____
_____

Where I went last night / details:

_____
_____

I drank:

_____
_____
_____

I got:

☐ Buzzed ☐ Wasted
☐ Tipsy ☐ Sh*t-faced
☐ Drunk ☐ Annihilated

I lost:

☐ Keys ☐ Phone ☐ Wallet ☐ Dignity ☐ Other _____

I can't believe I:

☐ Puked—How many times / where / on whom? _____
☐ Drunk dialed / texted / emailed _____
☐ Other awesomeness _____

HOOKUPS

Who: _____ ☐ No clue

Where: _____

Looks: ☆ ☆ ☆ ☆ ☆   ☐ Butt ugly   ☐ Doesn't matter
                                              ☐ Super hot   ☐ Beer goggles

Personality: ☆ ☆ ☆ ☆ ☆   ☐ Zero   ☐ Soul mate
                                              ☐ Just okay   ☐ Who cares

Details: **I think he/she looked like:**

_____

_____

_____

_____

_____

_____

How hot did it get?

☐ ZZZ   ☐ G   ☐ PG   ☐ PG-13   ☐ R   ☐ NC-17   ☐ X   ☐ XXX

Next steps?

☐ Avoid   ☐ Stalk   ☐ Go to church   ☐ Get tested   ☐ Hit that again

Note to self:

_____

_____

Remember to drink a glass of water for every glass of alcohol and drink more water before you go to bed. Coconut water is also super hydrating, as it contains essential electrolytes.

HANGOVERS

DATE

Hangover rating ☐ Still drunk

☐ A glass of water and good to go
☐ Greasy breakfast, please
☐ Throbbing headache
☐ Feeling pretty crappy

☐ Everything is spinning
☐ Afterparty in the bathroom
☐ Can't move / Never getting out of bed
☐ **Never** drinking again

Where did I wake up?

_____

☐ Alone ☐ With _____ ☐ WTF ☐ Walk of shame

The last thing I remember:

_____
_____

Where I went last night / details:

_____
_____

I drank:

_____

_____

_____

I got:

☐ Buzzed ☐ Wasted
☐ Tipsy ☐ Sh*t-faced
☐ Drunk ☐ Annihilated

I lost:

☐ Keys ☐ Phone ☐ Wallet ☐ Dignity ☐ Other _____

I can't believe I:

☐ Puked—How many times / where / on whom? _____
☐ Drunk dialed / texted / emailed _____
☐ Other awesomeness _____

HOOKUPS

Who: _____ ☐ No clue

Where: _____

Looks: ☆ ☆ ☆ ☆ ☆   ☐ Butt ugly   ☐ Doesn't matter
                          ☐ Super hot   ☐ Beer goggles

Personality: ☆ ☆ ☆ ☆ ☆   ☐ Zero   ☐ Soul mate
                                 ☐ Just okay   ☐ Who cares

Details: **I think he/she looked like:**

_____

_____

_____

_____

_____

_____

How hot did it get?

☐ ZZZ   ☐ G   ☐ PG   ☐ PG-13   ☐ R   ☐ NC-17   ☐ X   ☐ XXX

Next steps?

☐ Avoid   ☐ Stalk   ☐ Go to church   ☐ Get tested   ☐ Hit that again

Note to self:

_____

_____

Consider swapping your bourbon for vodka. Darker liquors contain more congeners, by-products of alcohol fermentation, which are believed to make hangovers worse.

HANGOVERS

Hangover rating ☐ Still drunk

☐ A glass of water and good to go
☐ Greasy breakfast, please
☐ Throbbing headache
☐ Feeling pretty crappy

☐ Everything is spinning
☐ Afterparty in the bathroom
☐ Can't move / Never getting out of bed
☐ **Never** drinking again

Where did I wake up?

_____

☐ Alone ☐ With _____ ☐ WTF ☐ Walk of shame

The last thing I remember:

_____
_____

Where I went last night / details:

_____
_____

I drank:

_____
_____
_____

I got:

☐ Buzzed ☐ Wasted
☐ Tipsy ☐ Sh*t-faced
☐ Drunk ☐ Annihilated

I lost:

☐ Keys ☐ Phone ☐ Wallet ☐ Dignity ☐ Other _____

I can't believe I:

☐ Puked—How many times / where / on whom? _____
☐ Drunk dialed / texted / emailed _____
☐ Other awesomeness _____

HOOKUPS

Who: _____ ☐ No clue

Where: _____

Looks: ☆ ☆ ☆ ☆ ☆   ☐ Butt ugly   ☐ Doesn't matter
                              ☐ Super hot   ☐ Beer goggles

Personality: ☆ ☆ ☆ ☆ ☆   ☐ Zero   ☐ Soul mate
                                    ☐ Just okay   ☐ Who cares

Details: **I think he/she looked like:**

_____

_____

_____

_____

_____

How hot did it get?

☐ ZZZ ☐ G ☐ PG ☐ PG-13 ☐ R ☐ NC-17 ☐ X ☐ XXX

Next steps?

☐ Avoid ☐ Stalk ☐ Go to church ☐ Get tested ☐ Hit that again

Note to self:

_____

_____

After a night of fun times, eat something before crawling into bed.
Bananas are a great choice—they contain potassium, which alcohol
consumption depletes from your body, and B_6, which is claimed to
be a great hangover killer.

HANGOVERS

Hangover rating ☐ Still drunk

☐ A glass of water and good to go
☐ Greasy breakfast, please
☐ Throbbing headache
☐ Feeling pretty crappy

☐ Everything is spinning
☐ Afterparty in the bathroom
☐ Can't move / Never getting out of bed
☐ **Never** drinking again

Where did I wake up?

_____

☐ Alone ☐ With _____ ☐ WTF ☐ Walk of shame

The last thing I remember:

_____
_____

Where I went last night / details:

_____
_____

I drank:

_____
_____
_____

I got:

☐ Buzzed   ☐ Wasted
☐ Tipsy   ☐ Sh*t-faced
☐ Drunk   ☐ Annihilated

I lost:

☐ Keys ☐ Phone ☐ Wallet ☐ Dignity ☐ Other _____

I can't believe I:

☐ Puked—How many times / where / on whom? _____
☐ Drunk dialed / texted / emailed _____
☐ Other awesomeness _____

HOOKUPS

Who: _____ ☐ No clue

Where: _____

Looks: ☆ ☆ ☆ ☆ ☆   ☐ Butt ugly   ☐ Doesn't matter
                                       ☐ Super hot   ☐ Beer goggles

Personality: ☆ ☆ ☆ ☆ ☆   ☐ Zero   ☐ Soul mate
                                             ☐ Just okay   ☐ Who cares

Details: **I think he/she looked like:**

_____

_____

_____

_____

_____

How hot did it get?
☐ ZZZ   ☐ G   ☐ PG   ☐ PG-13   ☐ R   ☐ NC-17   ☐ X   ☐ XXX

Next steps?
☐ Avoid   ☐ Stalk   ☐ Go to church   ☐ Get tested   ☐ Hit that again

Note to self:
_____

_____

> If you have friends who think it's funny to write on the passed-out person's forehead, remember to look in a mirror before you leave the house today.

HANGOVERS

Hangover rating ☐ Still drunk

☐ A glass of water and good to go
☐ Greasy breakfast, please
☐ Throbbing headache
☐ Feeling pretty crappy

☐ Everything is spinning
☐ Afterparty in the bathroom
☐ Can't move / Never getting out of bed
☐ **Never** drinking again

Where did I wake up?

_____

☐ Alone ☐ With _____ ☐ WTF ☐ Walk of shame

The last thing I remember:

_____
_____

Where I went last night / details:

_____
_____

I drank:

_____

_____

_____

I got:

☐ Buzzed   ☐ Wasted
☐ Tipsy   ☐ Sh*t-faced
☐ Drunk   ☐ Annihilated

I lost:

☐ Keys ☐ Phone ☐ Wallet ☐ Dignity ☐ Other _____

I can't believe I:

☐ Puked—How many times / where / on whom? _____

☐ Drunk dialed / texted / emailed _____

☐ Other awesomeness _____

HOOKUPS

Who: _____ ☐ No clue

Where: _____

Looks: ☆ ☆ ☆ ☆ ☆   ☐ Butt ugly   ☐ Doesn't matter
                                  ☐ Super hot   ☐ Beer goggles

Personality: ☆ ☆ ☆ ☆ ☆   ☐ Zero   ☐ Soul mate
                                          ☐ Just okay   ☐ Who cares

Details: **I think he/she looked like:**

_____

_____

_____

_____

_____

_____

How hot did it get?

☐ ZZZ ☐ G ☐ PG ☐ PG-13 ☐ R ☐ NC-17 ☐ X ☐ XXX

Next steps?

☐ Avoid ☐ Stalk ☐ Go to church ☐ Get tested ☐ Hit that again

Note to self:

_____

_____

You're not imagining it: Your hangovers really are getting worse. That's because as you age, you produce less alcohol dehydrogenase, the enzyme that breaks down alcohol.

HANGOVERS

Hangover rating ☐ Still drunk

☐ A glass of water and good to go
☐ Greasy breakfast, please
☐ Throbbing headache
☐ Feeling pretty crappy

☐ Everything is spinning
☐ Afterparty in the bathroom
☐ Can't move / Never getting out of bed
☐ **Never** drinking again

Where did I wake up?

_____

☐ Alone ☐ With _____ ☐ WTF ☐ Walk of shame

The last thing I remember:

_____

_____

Where I went last night / details:

_____

_____

I drank:

_____

_____

_____

I got:

☐ Buzzed ☐ Wasted
☐ Tipsy ☐ Sh*t-faced
☐ Drunk ☐ Annihilated

I lost:

☐ Keys ☐ Phone ☐ Wallet ☐ Dignity ☐ Other _____

I can't believe I:

☐ Puked—How many times / where / on whom? _____
☐ Drunk dialed / texted / emailed _____
☐ Other awesomeness _____

HOOKUPS

Who: _____ ☐ No clue

Where: _____

Looks: ☆ ☆ ☆ ☆ ☆   ☐ Butt ugly   ☐ Doesn't matter
                                  ☐ Super hot   ☐ Beer goggles

Personality: ☆ ☆ ☆ ☆ ☆   ☐ Zero   ☐ Soul mate
                                     ☐ Just okay   ☐ Who cares

Details: **I think he/she looked like:**

_____

_____

_____

_____

_____

How hot did it get?

☐ ZZZ   ☐ G   ☐ PG   ☐ PG-13   ☐ R   ☐ NC-17   ☐ X   ☐ XXX

Next steps?

☐ Avoid   ☐ Stalk   ☐ Go to church   ☐ Get tested   ☐ Hit that again

Note to self:

_____

_____

> Hey, drunky, put down the phone. Drunk dialing or texting always results in embarrassing apology dialing the next day.

HANGOVERS

DATE

Hangover rating ☐ Still drunk

☐ A glass of water and good to go
☐ Greasy breakfast, please
☐ Throbbing headache
☐ Feeling pretty crappy

☐ Everything is spinning
☐ Afterparty in the bathroom
☐ Can't move / Never getting out of bed
☐ **Never** drinking again

Where did I wake up?

_____

☐ Alone ☐ With _____ ☐ WTF ☐ Walk of shame

The last thing I remember:

_____

_____

Where I went last night / details:

_____

_____

I drank:

_____

_____

_____

I got:

☐ Buzzed ☐ Wasted
☐ Tipsy ☐ Sh*t-faced
☐ Drunk ☐ Annihilated

I lost:

☐ Keys ☐ Phone ☐ Wallet ☐ Dignity ☐ Other _____

I can't believe I:

☐ Puked—How many times / where / on whom? _____
☐ Drunk dialed / texted / emailed _____
☐ Other awesomeness _____

HOOKUPS

Who: _____ ☐ No clue

Where: _____

Looks: ☆ ☆ ☆ ☆ ☆   ☐ Butt ugly   ☐ Doesn't matter
                        ☐ Super hot   ☐ Beer goggles

Personality: ☆ ☆ ☆ ☆ ☆   ☐ Zero   ☐ Soul mate
                              ☐ Just okay   ☐ Who cares

Details: **I think he/she looked like:**

_____

_____

_____

_____

_____

_____

How hot did it get?

☐ ZZZ ☐ G ☐ PG ☐ PG-13 ☐ R ☐ NC-17 ☐ X ☐ XXX

Next steps?

☐ Avoid ☐ Stalk ☐ Go to church ☐ Get tested ☐ Hit that again

Note to self:

_____

_____

Sunglasses are essential for concealing bleary, hungover eyes and making the walk of shame a little less shameful.

HANGOVERS

Hangover rating ☐ Still drunk

☐ A glass of water and good to go
☐ Greasy breakfast, please
☐ Throbbing headache
☐ Feeling pretty crappy

☐ Everything is spinning
☐ Afterparty in the bathroom
☐ Can't move / Never getting out of bed
☐ **Never** drinking again

Where did I wake up?

_____

☐ Alone ☐ With _____ ☐ WTF ☐ Walk of shame

The last thing I remember:

_____

_____

Where I went last night / details:

_____

_____

I drank:

_____

_____

_____

I got:

☐ Buzzed ☐ Wasted
☐ Tipsy ☐ Sh*t-faced
☐ Drunk ☐ Annihilated

I lost:

☐ Keys ☐ Phone ☐ Wallet ☐ Dignity ☐ Other _____

I can't believe I:

☐ Puked—How many times / where / on whom? _____

☐ Drunk dialed / texted / emailed _____

☐ Other awesomeness _____

HOOKUPS

Who: _____ ☐ No clue

Where: _____

Looks: ☆ ☆ ☆ ☆ ☆   ☐ Butt ugly   ☐ Doesn't matter
                                    ☐ Super hot   ☐ Beer goggles

Personality: ☆ ☆ ☆ ☆ ☆   ☐ Zero   ☐ Soul mate
                                         ☐ Just okay   ☐ Who cares

Details: **I think he/she looked like:**

_____

_____

_____

_____

_____

How hot did it get?

☐ ZZZ   ☐ G   ☐ PG   ☐ PG-13   ☐ R   ☐ NC-17   ☐ X   ☐ XXX

Next steps?

☐ Avoid   ☐ Stalk   ☐ Go to church   ☐ Get tested   ☐ Hit that again

Note to self:

_____

_____

It's been said that drinking a glass of milk or a spoonful of olive oil before consuming alcohol can help prevent a hangover. The milk and oil coat the stomach lining and slow down the absorption of alcohol.

HANGOVERS

DATE

Hangover rating ☐ Still drunk

☐ A glass of water and good to go
☐ Greasy breakfast, please
☐ Throbbing headache
☐ Feeling pretty crappy

☐ Everything is spinning
☐ Afterparty in the bathroom
☐ Can't move / Never getting out of bed
☐ **Never** drinking again

Where did I wake up?

_____

☐ Alone ☐ With _____ ☐ WTF ☐ Walk of shame

The last thing I remember:

_____

_____

Where I went last night / details:

_____

_____

I drank:

_____

_____

_____

I got:

☐ Buzzed   ☐ Wasted
☐ Tipsy   ☐ Sh*t-faced
☐ Drunk   ☐ Annihilated

I lost:

☐ Keys ☐ Phone ☐ Wallet ☐ Dignity ☐ Other _____

I can't believe I:

☐ Puked—How many times / where / on whom? _____
☐ Drunk dialed / texted / emailed _____
☐ Other awesomeness _____

HOOKUPS

Who: _____ ☐ No clue

Where: _____

Looks: ☆ ☆ ☆ ☆ ☆   ☐ Butt ugly   ☐ Doesn't matter
                          ☐ Super hot   ☐ Beer goggles

Personality: ☆ ☆ ☆ ☆ ☆   ☐ Zero   ☐ Soul mate
                                ☐ Just okay   ☐ Who cares

Details: **I think he/she looked like:**

_____

_____

_____

_____

_____

How hot did it get?

☐ ZZZ   ☐ G   ☐ PG   ☐ PG-13   ☐ R   ☐ NC-17   ☐ X   ☐ XXX

Next steps?

☐ Avoid   ☐ Stalk   ☐ Go to church   ☐ Get tested   ☐ Hit that again

Note to self:

_____

_____

Remember to drink a glass of water for every glass of alcohol and drink more water before you go to bed. Coconut water is also super hydrating, as it contains essential electrolytes.

HANGOVERS

DATE

Hangover rating ☐ Still drunk

☐ A glass of water and good to go
☐ Greasy breakfast, please
☐ Throbbing headache
☐ Feeling pretty crappy

☐ Everything is spinning
☐ Afterparty in the bathroom
☐ Can't move / Never getting out of bed
☐ **Never** drinking again

Where did I wake up?

_____

☐ Alone ☐ With _____ ☐ WTF ☐ Walk of shame

The last thing I remember:

_____

_____

Where I went last night / details:

_____

_____

I drank:

_____

_____

_____

I got:

☐ Buzzed   ☐ Wasted
☐ Tipsy   ☐ Sh*t-faced
☐ Drunk   ☐ Annihilated

I lost:

☐ Keys ☐ Phone ☐ Wallet ☐ Dignity ☐ Other _____

I can't believe I:

☐ Puked—How many times / where / on whom? _____

☐ Drunk dialed / texted / emailed _____

☐ Other awesomeness _____

HOOKUPS

Who: _____ ☐ No clue

Where: _____

Looks: ☆ ☆ ☆ ☆ ☆   ☐ Butt ugly   ☐ Doesn't matter
                          ☐ Super hot   ☐ Beer goggles

Personality: ☆ ☆ ☆ ☆ ☆   ☐ Zero   ☐ Soul mate
                               ☐ Just okay   ☐ Who cares

Details: **I think he/she looked like:**

_____

_____

_____

_____

_____

How hot did it get?

☐ ZZZ ☐ G ☐ PG ☐ PG-13 ☐ R ☐ NC-17 ☐ X ☐ XXX

Next steps?

☐ Avoid ☐ Stalk ☐ Go to church ☐ Get tested ☐ Hit that again

Note to self:

_____

_____

Consider swapping your bourbon for vodka. Darker liquors contain more congeners, by-products of alcohol fermentation, which are believed to make hangovers worse.

HANGOVERS

Hangover rating   ☐ Still drunk

☐ A glass of water and good to go   ☐ Everything is spinning
☐ Greasy breakfast, please   ☐ Afterparty in the bathroom
☐ Throbbing headache   ☐ Can't move / Never getting out of bed
☐ Feeling pretty crappy   ☐ **Never** drinking again

Where did I wake up?

_____

☐ Alone   ☐ With _____   ☐ WTF   ☐ Walk of shame

The last thing I remember:

_____

_____

Where I went last night / details:

_____

I drank:

_____

_____

_____

I got:

☐ Buzzed   ☐ Wasted
☐ Tipsy   ☐ Sh*t-faced
☐ Drunk   ☐ Annihilated

I lost:

☐ Keys   ☐ Phone   ☐ Wallet   ☐ Dignity   ☐ Other _____

I can't believe I:

☐ Puked—How many times / where / on whom? _____
☐ Drunk dialed / texted / emailed _____
☐ Other awesomeness _____

HOOKUPS

Who: _____ ☐ No clue

Where: _____

Looks: ☆ ☆ ☆ ☆ ☆   ☐ Butt ugly   ☐ Doesn't matter
                          ☐ Super hot   ☐ Beer goggles

Personality: ☆ ☆ ☆ ☆ ☆   ☐ Zero   ☐ Soul mate
                               ☐ Just okay   ☐ Who cares

Details: **I think he/she looked like:**

_____

_____

_____

_____

_____

How hot did it get?

☐ ZZZ ☐ G ☐ PG ☐ PG-13 ☐ R ☐ NC-17 ☐ X ☐ XXX

Next steps?

☐ Avoid ☐ Stalk ☐ Go to church ☐ Get tested ☐ Hit that again

Note to self:

_____

_____

After a night of fun times, eat something before crawling into bed.
Bananas are a great choice—they contain potassium, which alcohol
consumption depletes from your body, and B_6, which is claimed to
be a great hangover killer.

HANGOVERS

Hangover rating   ☐ Still drunk

☐ A glass of water and good to go   ☐ Everything is spinning
☐ Greasy breakfast, please   ☐ Afterparty in the bathroom
☐ Throbbing headache   ☐ Can't move / Never getting out of bed
☐ Feeling pretty crappy   ☐ **Never** drinking again

Where did I wake up?

_____

☐ Alone   ☐ With _____   ☐ WTF   ☐ Walk of shame

The last thing I remember:

_____

_____

Where I went last night / details:

_____

_____

I drank:

_____

_____

_____

I got:

☐ Buzzed   ☐ Wasted
☐ Tipsy   ☐ Sh*t-faced
☐ Drunk   ☐ Annihilated

I lost:

☐ Keys   ☐ Phone   ☐ Wallet   ☐ Dignity   ☐ Other _____

I can't believe I:

☐ Puked—How many times / where / on whom? _____

☐ Drunk dialed / texted / emailed _____

☐ Other awesomeness _____

HOOKUPS

Who: _____ ☐ No clue

Where: _____

Looks: ☆ ☆ ☆ ☆ ☆　　☐ Butt ugly　　☐ Doesn't matter
　　　　　　　　　　　　☐ Super hot　　☐ Beer goggles

Personality: ☆ ☆ ☆ ☆ ☆　　☐ Zero　　　☐ Soul mate
　　　　　　　　　　　　　　　☐ Just okay　☐ Who cares

Details:　　　　　　　　　　　　**I think he/she looked like:**

_____

_____

_____

_____

_____

_____

How hot did it get?

☐ ZZZ　☐ G　☐ PG　☐ PG-13　☐ R　☐ NC-17　☐ X　☐ XXX

Next steps?

☐ Avoid　☐ Stalk　☐ Go to church　☐ Get tested　☐ Hit that again

Note to self:

_____

_____

If you have friends who think it's funny to write on the passed-out person's forehead, remember to look in a mirror before you leave the house today.

HANGOVERS

DATE

Hangover rating ☐ Still drunk

☐ A glass of water and good to go
☐ Greasy breakfast, please
☐ Throbbing headache
☐ Feeling pretty crappy

☐ Everything is spinning
☐ Afterparty in the bathroom
☐ Can't move / Never getting out of bed
☐ **Never** drinking again

Where did I wake up?

_____

☐ Alone ☐ With _____ ☐ WTF ☐ Walk of shame

The last thing I remember:

_____
_____

Where I went last night / details:

_____
_____

I drank:

_____
_____
_____

I got:

☐ Buzzed ☐ Wasted
☐ Tipsy ☐ Sh*t-faced
☐ Drunk ☐ Annihilated

I lost:

☐ Keys ☐ Phone ☐ Wallet ☐ Dignity ☐ Other _____

I can't believe I:

☐ Puked—How many times / where / on whom? _____
☐ Drunk dialed / texted / emailed _____
☐ Other awesomeness _____

HOOKUPS

Who: _____ ☐ No clue

Where: _____

Looks: ☆ ☆ ☆ ☆ ☆   ☐ Butt ugly   ☐ Doesn't matter
                                       ☐ Super hot   ☐ Beer goggles

Personality: ☆ ☆ ☆ ☆ ☆   ☐ Zero   ☐ Soul mate
                                         ☐ Just okay   ☐ Who cares

Details: **I think he/she looked like:**

_____

_____

_____

_____

_____

_____

How hot did it get?

☐ ZZZ   ☐ G   ☐ PG   ☐ PG-13   ☐ R   ☐ NC-17   ☐ X   ☐ XXX

Next steps?

☐ Avoid   ☐ Stalk   ☐ Go to church   ☐ Get tested   ☐ Hit that again

Note to self:

_____

_____

> You're not imagining it: Your hangovers really are getting worse. That's because as you age, you produce less alcohol dehydrogenase, the enzyme that breaks down alcohol.

HANGOVERS

DATE

Hangover rating ☐ Still drunk

☐ A glass of water and good to go
☐ Greasy breakfast, please
☐ Throbbing headache
☐ Feeling pretty crappy

☐ Everything is spinning
☐ Afterparty in the bathroom
☐ Can't move / Never getting out of bed
☐ **Never** drinking again

Where did I wake up?

_____

☐ Alone ☐ With _____ ☐ WTF ☐ Walk of shame

The last thing I remember:

_____
_____

Where I went last night / details:

_____
_____

I drank:

_____
_____
_____

I got:

☐ Buzzed ☐ Wasted
☐ Tipsy ☐ Sh*t-faced
☐ Drunk ☐ Annihilated

I lost:

☐ Keys ☐ Phone ☐ Wallet ☐ Dignity ☐ Other _____

I can't believe I:

☐ Puked—How many times / where / on whom? _____
☐ Drunk dialed / texted / emailed _____
☐ Other awesomeness _____
_____

HOOKUPS

Who: _____ ☐ No clue

Where: _____

Looks: ☆ ☆ ☆ ☆ ☆   ☐ Butt ugly   ☐ Doesn't matter
                              ☐ Super hot   ☐ Beer goggles

Personality: ☆ ☆ ☆ ☆ ☆   ☐ Zero   ☐ Soul mate
                                  ☐ Just okay   ☐ Who cares

Details: **I think he/she looked like:**

_____

_____

_____

_____

_____

_____

How hot did it get?
☐ ZZZ ☐ G ☐ PG ☐ PG-13 ☐ R ☐ NC-17 ☐ X ☐ XXX

Next steps?
☐ Avoid ☐ Stalk ☐ Go to church ☐ Get tested ☐ Hit that again

Note to self:

_____

_____

Hey, drunky, put down the phone. Drunk dialing or texting always results in embarrassing apology dialing the next day.

HANGOVERS

DATE

Hangover rating ☐ Still drunk

☐ A glass of water and good to go
☐ Greasy breakfast, please
☐ Throbbing headache
☐ Feeling pretty crappy

☐ Everything is spinning
☐ Afterparty in the bathroom
☐ Can't move / Never getting out of bed
☐ **Never** drinking again

Where did I wake up?

_____

☐ Alone ☐ With _____ ☐ WTF ☐ Walk of shame

The last thing I remember:

_____

_____

Where I went last night / details:

_____

_____

I drank:

_____

_____

_____

I got:

☐ Buzzed ☐ Wasted
☐ Tipsy ☐ Sh*t-faced
☐ Drunk ☐ Annihilated

I lost:

☐ Keys ☐ Phone ☐ Wallet ☐ Dignity ☐ Other _____

I can't believe I:

☐ Puked—How many times / where / on whom? _____
☐ Drunk dialed / texted / emailed _____
☐ Other awesomeness _____

_____

HOOKUPS

Who: _____ ☐ No clue

Where: _____

Looks: ☆ ☆ ☆ ☆ ☆   ☐ Butt ugly   ☐ Doesn't matter
                           ☐ Super hot   ☐ Beer goggles

Personality: ☆ ☆ ☆ ☆ ☆   ☐ Zero   ☐ Soul mate
                                ☐ Just okay   ☐ Who cares

Details: **I think he/she looked like:**

_____

_____

_____

_____

_____

_____

How hot did it get?

☐ ZZZ   ☐ G   ☐ PG   ☐ PG-13   ☐ R   ☐ NC-17   ☐ X   ☐ XXX

Next steps?

☐ Avoid   ☐ Stalk   ☐ Go to church   ☐ Get tested   ☐ Hit that again

Note to self:

_____

_____

Sunglasses are essential for concealing bleary, hungover eyes and making
the walk of shame a little less shameful.

HANGOVERS

Hangover rating ☐ Still drunk

☐ A glass of water and good to go
☐ Greasy breakfast, please
☐ Throbbing headache
☐ Feeling pretty crappy

☐ Everything is spinning
☐ Afterparty in the bathroom
☐ Can't move / Never getting out of bed
☐ **Never** drinking again

Where did I wake up?

_____

☐ Alone ☐ With _____ ☐ WTF ☐ Walk of shame

The last thing I remember:

_____

_____

Where I went last night / details:

_____

_____

I drank:

_____

_____

_____

I got:

☐ Buzzed   ☐ Wasted
☐ Tipsy   ☐ Sh*t-faced
☐ Drunk   ☐ Annihilated

I lost:

☐ Keys ☐ Phone ☐ Wallet ☐ Dignity ☐ Other _____

I can't believe I:

☐ Puked—How many times / where / on whom? _____
☐ Drunk dialed / texted / emailed _____
☐ Other awesomeness _____

HOOKUPS

Who: _____ ☐ No clue

Where: _____

Looks: ☆ ☆ ☆ ☆ ☆   ☐ Butt ugly   ☐ Doesn't matter
                              ☐ Super hot   ☐ Beer goggles

Personality: ☆ ☆ ☆ ☆ ☆   ☐ Zero   ☐ Soul mate
                                   ☐ Just okay   ☐ Who cares

Details: **I think he/she looked like:**

_____

_____

_____

_____

_____

_____

How hot did it get?

☐ ZZZ   ☐ G   ☐ PG   ☐ PG-13   ☐ R   ☐ NC-17   ☐ X   ☐ XXX

Next steps?

☐ Avoid   ☐ Stalk   ☐ Go to church   ☐ Get tested   ☐ Hit that again

Note to self:

_____

_____

It's been said that drinking a glass of milk or a spoonful of olive oil before
consuming alcohol can help prevent a hangover. The milk and oil coat the
stomach lining and slow down the absorption of alcohol.

HANGOVERS

DATE

Hangover rating ☐ Still drunk

☐ A glass of water and good to go
☐ Greasy breakfast, please
☐ Throbbing headache
☐ Feeling pretty crappy

☐ Everything is spinning
☐ Afterparty in the bathroom
☐ Can't move / Never getting out of bed
☐ **Never** drinking again

Where did I wake up?

_____

☐ Alone ☐ With _____ ☐ WTF ☐ Walk of shame

The last thing I remember:

_____
_____

Where I went last night / details:

_____
_____

I drank:

_____
_____
_____

I got:

☐ Buzzed ☐ Wasted
☐ Tipsy ☐ Sh*t-faced
☐ Drunk ☐ Annihilated

I lost:

☐ Keys ☐ Phone ☐ Wallet ☐ Dignity ☐ Other _____

I can't believe I:

☐ Puked—How many times / where / on whom? _____
☐ Drunk dialed / texted / emailed _____
☐ Other awesomeness _____

HOOKUPS

Who: _____ ☐ No clue

Where: _____

Looks: ☆ ☆ ☆ ☆ ☆   ☐ Butt ugly   ☐ Doesn't matter
☐ Super hot   ☐ Beer goggles

Personality: ☆ ☆ ☆ ☆ ☆   ☐ Zero   ☐ Soul mate
☐ Just okay   ☐ Who cares

Details:

_____

_____

_____

_____

_____

_____

I think he/she looked like:

How hot did it get?

☐ ZZZ ☐ G ☐ PG ☐ PG-13 ☐ R ☐ NC-17 ☐ X ☐ XXX

Next steps?

☐ Avoid ☐ Stalk ☐ Go to church ☐ Get tested ☐ Hit that again

Note to self:

_____

_____

Remember to drink a glass of water for every glass of alcohol and drink more water before you go to bed. Coconut water is also super hydrating, as it contains essential electrolytes.

HANGOVERS

DATE

Hangover rating ☐ Still drunk

☐ A glass of water and good to go
☐ Greasy breakfast, please
☐ Throbbing headache
☐ Feeling pretty crappy

☐ Everything is spinning
☐ Afterparty in the bathroom
☐ Can't move / Never getting out of bed
☐ **Never** drinking again

Where did I wake up?

_____

☐ Alone ☐ With _____ ☐ WTF ☐ Walk of shame

The last thing I remember:

_____
_____

Where I went last night / details:

_____
_____

I drank:

_____
_____
_____

I got:

☐ Buzzed ☐ Wasted
☐ Tipsy ☐ Sh*t-faced
☐ Drunk ☐ Annihilated

I lost:

☐ Keys ☐ Phone ☐ Wallet ☐ Dignity ☐ Other _____

I can't believe I:

☐ Puked—How many times / where / on whom? _____
☐ Drunk dialed / texted / emailed _____
☐ Other awesomeness _____

HOOKUPS

Who: _____ ☐ No clue

Where: _____

Looks: ☆ ☆ ☆ ☆ ☆   ☐ Butt ugly   ☐ Doesn't matter
                           ☐ Super hot   ☐ Beer goggles

Personality: ☆ ☆ ☆ ☆ ☆   ☐ Zero   ☐ Soul mate
                               ☐ Just okay   ☐ Who cares

Details: **I think he/she looked like:**

_____

_____

_____

_____

_____

_____

How hot did it get?

☐ ZZZ   ☐ G   ☐ PG   ☐ PG-13   ☐ R   ☐ NC-17   ☐ X   ☐ XXX

Next steps?

☐ Avoid   ☐ Stalk   ☐ Go to church   ☐ Get tested   ☐ Hit that again

Note to self:

_____

_____

> Consider swapping your bourbon for vodka. Darker liquors contain more congeners, by-products of alcohol fermentation, which are believed to make hangovers worse.

HANGOVERS

DATE

Hangover rating ☐ Still drunk

☐ A glass of water and good to go
☐ Greasy breakfast, please
☐ Throbbing headache
☐ Feeling pretty crappy

☐ Everything is spinning
☐ Afterparty in the bathroom
☐ Can't move / Never getting out of bed
☐ **Never** drinking again

Where did I wake up?

☐ Alone ☐ With _____ ☐ WTF ☐ Walk of shame

The last thing I remember:

Where I went last night / details:

I drank:	I got:	
	☐ Buzzed	☐ Wasted
	☐ Tipsy	☐ Sh*t-faced
	☐ Drunk	☐ Annihilated

I lost:

☐ Keys ☐ Phone ☐ Wallet ☐ Dignity ☐ Other _____

I can't believe I:

☐ Puked—How many times / where / on whom? _____
☐ Drunk dialed / texted / emailed _____
☐ Other awesomeness _____

HOOKUPS

Who: _____ ☐ No clue

Where: _____

Looks: ☆ ☆ ☆ ☆ ☆   ☐ Butt ugly   ☐ Doesn't matter
                                ☐ Super hot   ☐ Beer goggles

Personality: ☆ ☆ ☆ ☆ ☆   ☐ Zero   ☐ Soul mate
                                      ☐ Just okay   ☐ Who cares

Details: **I think he/she looked like:**

_____

_____

_____

_____

_____

_____

How hot did it get?

☐ ZZZ ☐ G ☐ PG ☐ PG-13 ☐ R ☐ NC-17 ☐ X ☐ XXX

Next steps?

☐ Avoid ☐ Stalk ☐ Go to church ☐ Get tested ☐ Hit that again

Note to self:

_____

_____

After a night of fun times, eat something before crawling into bed.
Bananas are a great choice—they contain potassium, which alcohol
consumption depletes from your body, and B_6, which is claimed to
be a great hangover killer.

HANGOVERS

Hangover rating ☐ Still drunk

☐ A glass of water and good to go
☐ Greasy breakfast, please
☐ Throbbing headache
☐ Feeling pretty crappy

☐ Everything is spinning
☐ Afterparty in the bathroom
☐ Can't move / Never getting out of bed
☐ **Never** drinking again

Where did I wake up?

_____

☐ Alone ☐ With _____ ☐ WTF ☐ Walk of shame

The last thing I remember:

_____
_____

Where I went last night / details:

_____
_____

I drank:

_____
_____
_____

I got:

☐ Buzzed ☐ Wasted
☐ Tipsy   ☐ Sh*t-faced
☐ Drunk   ☐ Annihilated

I lost:

☐ Keys ☐ Phone ☐ Wallet ☐ Dignity ☐ Other _____

I can't believe I:

☐ Puked—How many times / where / on whom? _____
☐ Drunk dialed / texted / emailed _____
☐ Other awesomeness _____

HOOKUPS

Who: _____ ☐ No clue

Where: _____

Looks: ☆ ☆ ☆ ☆ ☆   ☐ Butt ugly   ☐ Doesn't matter
                          ☐ Super hot   ☐ Beer goggles

Personality: ☆ ☆ ☆ ☆ ☆   ☐ Zero   ☐ Soul mate
                               ☐ Just okay   ☐ Who cares

Details: **I think he/she looked like:**

_____

_____

_____

_____

_____

_____

How hot did it get?

☐ ZZZ ☐ G ☐ PG ☐ PG-13 ☐ R ☐ NC-17 ☐ X ☐ XXX

Next steps?

☐ Avoid ☐ Stalk ☐ Go to church ☐ Get tested ☐ Hit that again

Note to self:

_____

_____

If you have friends who think it's funny to write on the passed-out
person's forehead, remember to look in a mirror before you leave the
house today.

HANGOVERS

Hangover rating ☐ Still drunk

☐ A glass of water and good to go   ☐ Everything is spinning
☐ Greasy breakfast, please   ☐ Afterparty in the bathroom
☐ Throbbing headache   ☐ Can't move / Never getting out of bed
☐ Feeling pretty crappy   ☐ **Never** drinking again

Where did I wake up?

_____

☐ Alone ☐ With _____ ☐ WTF ☐ Walk of shame

The last thing I remember:

_____

_____

Where I went last night / details:

_____

_____

I drank:

_____

_____

_____

I got:

☐ Buzzed   ☐ Wasted
☐ Tipsy   ☐ Sh*t-faced
☐ Drunk   ☐ Annihilated

I lost:

☐ Keys ☐ Phone ☐ Wallet ☐ Dignity ☐ Other _____

I can't believe I:

☐ Puked—How many times / where / on whom? _____
☐ Drunk dialed / texted / emailed _____
☐ Other awesomeness _____

HOOKUPS

Who: _____ ☐ No clue

Where: _____

Looks: ☆ ☆ ☆ ☆ ☆   ☐ Butt ugly   ☐ Doesn't matter
☐ Super hot   ☐ Beer goggles

Personality: ☆ ☆ ☆ ☆ ☆   ☐ Zero   ☐ Soul mate
☐ Just okay   ☐ Who cares

Details: **I think he/she looked like:**

_____

_____

_____

_____

_____

_____

How hot did it get?

☐ ZZZ   ☐ G   ☐ PG   ☐ PG-13   ☐ R   ☐ NC-17   ☐ X   ☐ XXX

Next steps?

☐ Avoid   ☐ Stalk   ☐ Go to church   ☐ Get tested   ☐ Hit that again

Note to self:

_____

_____

You're not imagining it: Your hangovers really are getting worse. That's
because as you age, you produce less alcohol dehydrogenase, the
enzyme that breaks down alcohol.

HANGOVERS

Hangover rating   ☐ Still drunk

☐ A glass of water and good to go
☐ Greasy breakfast, please
☐ Throbbing headache
☐ Feeling pretty crappy

☐ Everything is spinning
☐ Afterparty in the bathroom
☐ Can't move / Never getting out of bed
☐ **Never** drinking again

Where did I wake up?

_____

☐ Alone ☐ With _____ ☐ WTF ☐ Walk of shame

The last thing I remember:

_____
_____

Where I went last night / details:

_____
_____

I drank:

_____
_____
_____

I got:

☐ Buzzed   ☐ Wasted
☐ Tipsy   ☐ Sh*t-faced
☐ Drunk   ☐ Annihilated

I lost:

☐ Keys ☐ Phone ☐ Wallet ☐ Dignity ☐ Other _____

I can't believe I:

☐ Puked—How many times / where / on whom? _____
☐ Drunk dialed / texted / emailed _____
☐ Other awesomeness _____

HOOKUPS

Who: _____ ☐ No clue

Where: _____

Looks: ☆ ☆ ☆ ☆ ☆   ☐ Butt ugly   ☐ Doesn't matter
                              ☐ Super hot   ☐ Beer goggles

Personality: ☆ ☆ ☆ ☆ ☆   ☐ Zero   ☐ Soul mate
                                    ☐ Just okay   ☐ Who cares

Details: **I think he/she looked like:**

_____

_____

_____

_____

_____

_____

How hot did it get?

☐ ZZZ ☐ G ☐ PG ☐ PG-13 ☐ R ☐ NC-17 ☐ X ☐ XXX

Next steps?

☐ Avoid ☐ Stalk ☐ Go to church ☐ Get tested ☐ Hit that again

Note to self:

_____

_____

Hey, drunky, put down the phone. Drunk dialing or texting always results in embarrassing apology dialing the next day.

HANGOVERS

Hangover rating ☐ Still drunk

☐ A glass of water and good to go
☐ Greasy breakfast, please
☐ Throbbing headache
☐ Feeling pretty crappy

☐ Everything is spinning
☐ Afterparty in the bathroom
☐ Can't move / Never getting out of bed
☐ **Never** drinking again

Where did I wake up?

_____

☐ Alone ☐ With _____ ☐ WTF ☐ Walk of shame

The last thing I remember:

_____
_____

Where I went last night / details:

_____
_____

I drank:

_____
_____
_____

I got:

☐ Buzzed   ☐ Wasted
☐ Tipsy   ☐ Sh*t-faced
☐ Drunk   ☐ Annihilated

I lost:

☐ Keys ☐ Phone ☐ Wallet ☐ Dignity ☐ Other _____

I can't believe I:

☐ Puked—How many times / where / on whom? _____
☐ Drunk dialed / texted / emailed _____
☐ Other awesomeness _____

HOOKUPS

Who: _____ ☐ No clue

Where: _____

Looks: ☆ ☆ ☆ ☆ ☆   ☐ Butt ugly   ☐ Doesn't matter
                                 ☐ Super hot   ☐ Beer goggles

Personality: ☆ ☆ ☆ ☆ ☆   ☐ Zero   ☐ Soul mate
                                      ☐ Just okay   ☐ Who cares

Details: **I think he/she looked like:**

_____

_____

_____

_____

_____

_____

How hot did it get?

☐ ZZZ   ☐ G   ☐ PG   ☐ PG-13   ☐ R   ☐ NC-17   ☐ X   ☐ XXX

Next steps?

☐ Avoid   ☐ Stalk   ☐ Go to church   ☐ Get tested   ☐ Hit that again

Note to self:

_____

_____

Sunglasses are essential for concealing bleary, hungover eyes and making the walk of shame a little less shameful.

HANGOVERS

DATE

Hangover rating ☐ Still drunk

☐ A glass of water and good to go
☐ Greasy breakfast, please
☐ Throbbing headache
☐ Feeling pretty crappy

☐ Everything is spinning
☐ Afterparty in the bathroom
☐ Can't move / Never getting out of bed
☐ **Never** drinking again

Where did I wake up?

_____

☐ Alone ☐ With _____ ☐ WTF ☐ Walk of shame

The last thing I remember:

_____
_____

Where I went last night / details:

_____
_____

I drank:

_____
_____
_____

I got:

☐ Buzzed ☐ Wasted
☐ Tipsy ☐ Sh*t-faced
☐ Drunk ☐ Annihilated

I lost:

☐ Keys ☐ Phone ☐ Wallet ☐ Dignity ☐ Other _____

I can't believe I:

☐ Puked—How many times / where / on whom? _____
☐ Drunk dialed / texted / emailed _____
☐ Other awesomeness _____

HOOKUPS

Who: _____ ☐ No clue

Where: _____

Looks: ☆ ☆ ☆ ☆ ☆   ☐ Butt ugly   ☐ Doesn't matter
                          ☐ Super hot   ☐ Beer goggles

Personality: ☆ ☆ ☆ ☆ ☆   ☐ Zero   ☐ Soul mate
                               ☐ Just okay   ☐ Who cares

Details: **I think he/she looked like:**

_____
_____
_____
_____   SKETCH HERE
_____
_____

How hot did it get?

☐ ZZZ ☐ G ☐ PG ☐ PG-13 ☐ R ☐ NC-17 ☐ X ☐ XXX

Next steps?

☐ Avoid ☐ Stalk ☐ Go to church ☐ Get tested ☐ Hit that again

Note to self:

_____
_____

> It's been said that drinking a glass of milk or a spoonful of olive oil before consuming alcohol can help prevent a hangover. The milk and oil coat the stomach lining and slow down the absorption of alcohol.

HANGOVERS

Hangover rating ☐ Still drunk

☐ A glass of water and good to go
☐ Greasy breakfast, please
☐ Throbbing headache
☐ Feeling pretty crappy

☐ Everything is spinning
☐ Afterparty in the bathroom
☐ Can't move / Never getting out of bed
☐ **Never** drinking again

Where did I wake up?

_____

☐ Alone ☐ With _____ ☐ WTF ☐ Walk of shame

The last thing I remember:

_____

_____

Where I went last night / details:

_____

_____

I drank:

_____

_____

_____

I got:

☐ Buzzed ☐ Wasted
☐ Tipsy ☐ Sh*t-faced
☐ Drunk ☐ Annihilated

I lost:

☐ Keys ☐ Phone ☐ Wallet ☐ Dignity ☐ Other _____

I can't believe I:

☐ Puked—How many times / where / on whom? _____

☐ Drunk dialed / texted / emailed _____

☐ Other awesomeness _____

HOOKUPS

Who: _____ ☐ No clue

Where: _____

Looks: ☆ ☆ ☆ ☆ ☆   ☐ Butt ugly   ☐ Doesn't matter
                          ☐ Super hot   ☐ Beer goggles

Personality: ☆ ☆ ☆ ☆ ☆   ☐ Zero   ☐ Soul mate
                               ☐ Just okay ☐ Who cares

Details: **I think he/she looked like:**

_____

_____

_____

_____

_____

_____

How hot did it get?

☐ ZZZ ☐ G ☐ PG ☐ PG-13 ☐ R ☐ NC-17 ☐ X ☐ XXX

Next steps?

☐ Avoid ☐ Stalk ☐ Go to church ☐ Get tested ☐ Hit that again

Note to self:

_____

_____

Remember to drink a glass of water for every glass of alcohol and drink
more water before you go to bed. Coconut water is also super hydrating,
as it contains essential electrolytes.

HANGOVERS

Hangover rating ☐ Still drunk

☐ A glass of water and good to go   ☐ Everything is spinning
☐ Greasy breakfast, please   ☐ Afterparty in the bathroom
☐ Throbbing headache   ☐ Can't move / Never getting out of bed
☐ Feeling pretty crappy   ☐ **Never** drinking again

Where did I wake up?

_____

☐ Alone ☐ With _____ ☐ WTF ☐ Walk of shame

The last thing I remember:

_____

_____

Where I went last night / details:

_____

_____

I drank:

_____

_____

_____

I got:

☐ Buzzed   ☐ Wasted
☐ Tipsy   ☐ Sh*t-faced
☐ Drunk   ☐ Annihilated

I lost:

☐ Keys ☐ Phone ☐ Wallet ☐ Dignity ☐ Other _____

I can't believe I:

☐ Puked—How many times / where / on whom? _____

☐ Drunk dialed / texted / emailed _____

☐ Other awesomeness _____

HOOKUPS

Who: _____ ☐ No clue

Where: _____

Looks: ☆ ☆ ☆ ☆ ☆   ☐ Butt ugly   ☐ Doesn't matter
                       ☐ Super hot   ☐ Beer goggles

Personality: ☆ ☆ ☆ ☆ ☆   ☐ Zero   ☐ Soul mate
                             ☐ Just okay   ☐ Who cares

Details: **I think he/she looked like:**

_____

_____

_____

_____

_____

_____

How hot did it get?

☐ ZZZ ☐ G ☐ PG ☐ PG-13 ☐ R ☐ NC-17 ☐ X ☐ XXX

Next steps?

☐ Avoid ☐ Stalk ☐ Go to church ☐ Get tested ☐ Hit that again

Note to self:

_____

_____

Consider swapping your bourbon for vodka. Darker liquors contain more congeners, by-products of alcohol fermentation, which are believed to make hangovers worse.

HANGOVERS

DATE

Hangover rating ☐ Still drunk

☐ A glass of water and good to go
☐ Greasy breakfast, please
☐ Throbbing headache
☐ Feeling pretty crappy

☐ Everything is spinning
☐ Afterparty in the bathroom
☐ Can't move/Never getting out of bed
☐ **Never** drinking again

Where did I wake up?

_____

☐ Alone ☐ With _____ ☐ WTF ☐ Walk of shame

The last thing I remember:

_____
_____

Where I went last night / details:

_____
_____

I drank:

_____
_____
_____

I got:

☐ Buzzed ☐ Wasted
☐ Tipsy ☐ Sh*t-faced
☐ Drunk ☐ Annihilated

I lost:

☐ Keys ☐ Phone ☐ Wallet ☐ Dignity ☐ Other _____

I can't believe I:

☐ Puked—How many times / where / on whom? _____
☐ Drunk dialed / texted / emailed _____
☐ Other awesomeness _____

HOOKUPS

Who: _____ ☐ No clue

Where: _____

Looks: ☆ ☆ ☆ ☆ ☆   ☐ Butt ugly   ☐ Doesn't matter
                                ☐ Super hot   ☐ Beer goggles

Personality: ☆ ☆ ☆ ☆ ☆   ☐ Zero   ☐ Soul mate
                                       ☐ Just okay   ☐ Who cares

Details: **I think he/she looked like:**

_____

_____

_____

_____

_____

How hot did it get?

☐ ZZZ   ☐ G   ☐ PG   ☐ PG-13   ☐ R   ☐ NC-17   ☐ X   ☐ XXX

Next steps?

☐ Avoid   ☐ Stalk   ☐ Go to church   ☐ Get tested   ☐ Hit that again

Note to self:

_____

_____

After a night of fun times, eat something before crawling into bed.
Bananas are a great choice—they contain potassium, which alcohol
consumption depletes from your body, and B_6, which is claimed to
be a great hangover killer.

HANGOVERS

DATE

Hangover rating ☐ Still drunk

☐ A glass of water and good to go
☐ Greasy breakfast, please
☐ Throbbing headache
☐ Feeling pretty crappy

☐ Everything is spinning
☐ Afterparty in the bathroom
☐ Can't move / Never getting out of bed
☐ **Never** drinking again

Where did I wake up?

_____

☐ Alone ☐ With _____ ☐ WTF ☐ Walk of shame

The last thing I remember:

_____
_____

Where I went last night / details:

_____
_____

I drank:

_____
_____
_____

I got:

☐ Buzzed   ☐ Wasted
☐ Tipsy   ☐ Sh*t-faced
☐ Drunk   ☐ Annihilated

I lost:

☐ Keys ☐ Phone ☐ Wallet ☐ Dignity ☐ Other _____

I can't believe I:

☐ Puked—How many times / where / on whom? _____
☐ Drunk dialed / texted / emailed _____
☐ Other awesomeness _____
_____

HOOKUPS

Who: _____ ☐ No clue

Where: _____

Looks: ☆ ☆ ☆ ☆ ☆ ☐ Butt ugly ☐ Doesn't matter
☐ Super hot ☐ Beer goggles

Personality: ☆ ☆ ☆ ☆ ☆ ☐ Zero ☐ Soul mate
☐ Just okay ☐ Who cares

Details:

_____

_____

_____

_____

_____

_____

I think he/she looked like:

How hot did it get?

☐ ZZZ ☐ G ☐ PG ☐ PG-13 ☐ R ☐ NC-17 ☐ X ☐ XXX

Next steps?

☐ Avoid ☐ Stalk ☐ Go to church ☐ Get tested ☐ Hit that again

Note to self:

_____

_____

If you have friends who think it's funny to write on the passed-out person's forehead, remember to look in a mirror before you leave the house today.

HANGOVERS

Hangover rating ☐ Still drunk

☐ A glass of water and good to go
☐ Greasy breakfast, please
☐ Throbbing headache
☐ Feeling pretty crappy

☐ Everything is spinning
☐ Afterparty in the bathroom
☐ Can't move / Never getting out of bed
☐ **Never** drinking again

Where did I wake up?

_____

☐ Alone ☐ With _____ ☐ WTF ☐ Walk of shame

The last thing I remember:

_____

_____

Where I went last night / details:

_____

_____

I drank:

_____

_____

_____

I got:

☐ Buzzed   ☐ Wasted
☐ Tipsy   ☐ Sh*t-faced
☐ Drunk   ☐ Annihilated

I lost:

☐ Keys ☐ Phone ☐ Wallet ☐ Dignity ☐ Other _____

I can't believe I:

☐ Puked—How many times / where / on whom? _____
☐ Drunk dialed / texted / emailed _____
☐ Other awesomeness _____

HOOKUPS

Who: _____ ☐ No clue

Where: _____

Looks: ☆ ☆ ☆ ☆ ☆   ☐ Butt ugly   ☐ Doesn't matter
                                      ☐ Super hot   ☐ Beer goggles

Personality: ☆ ☆ ☆ ☆ ☆   ☐ Zero   ☐ Soul mate
                                              ☐ Just okay   ☐ Who cares

Details: **I think he/she looked like:**

_____

_____

_____

_____

_____

_____

How hot did it get?

☐ ZZZ   ☐ G   ☐ PG   ☐ PG-13   ☐ R   ☐ NC-17   ☐ X   ☐ XXX

Next steps?

☐ Avoid   ☐ Stalk   ☐ Go to church   ☐ Get tested   ☐ Hit that again

Note to self:

_____

_____

> You're not imagining it: Your hangovers really are getting worse. That's because as you age, you produce less alcohol dehydrogenase, the enzyme that breaks down alcohol.

HANGOVERS

Hangover rating ☐ Still drunk

☐ A glass of water and good to go
☐ Greasy breakfast, please
☐ Throbbing headache
☐ Feeling pretty crappy

☐ Everything is spinning
☐ Afterparty in the bathroom
☐ Can't move / Never getting out of bed
☐ **Never** drinking again

Where did I wake up?

_____

☐ Alone ☐ With _____ ☐ WTF ☐ Walk of shame

The last thing I remember:

_____

_____

Where I went last night / details:

_____

_____

I drank:

_____

_____

_____

I got:

☐ Buzzed ☐ Wasted
☐ Tipsy ☐ Sh*t-faced
☐ Drunk ☐ Annihilated

I lost:

☐ Keys ☐ Phone ☐ Wallet ☐ Dignity ☐ Other _____

I can't believe I:

☐ Puked—How many times / where / on whom? _____
☐ Drunk dialed / texted / emailed _____
☐ Other awesomeness _____

_____

HOOKUPS

Who: _____ ☐ No clue

Where: _____

Looks: ☆ ☆ ☆ ☆ ☆   ☐ Butt ugly   ☐ Doesn't matter
                               ☐ Super hot   ☐ Beer goggles

Personality: ☆ ☆ ☆ ☆ ☆   ☐ Zero   ☐ Soul mate
                                     ☐ Just okay   ☐ Who cares

Details: **I think he/she looked like:**

_____

_____

_____

_____

_____

_____

How hot did it get?

☐ ZZZ ☐ G ☐ PG ☐ PG-13 ☐ R ☐ NC-17 ☐ X ☐ XXX

Next steps?

☐ Avoid ☐ Stalk ☐ Go to church ☐ Get tested ☐ Hit that again

Note to self:

_____

_____

Hey, drunky, put down the phone. Drunk dialing or texting always results in embarrassing apology dialing the next day.

HANGOVERS

DATE

Hangover rating
☐ Still drunk

☐ A glass of water and good to go
☐ Greasy breakfast, please
☐ Throbbing headache
☐ Feeling pretty crappy

☐ Everything is spinning
☐ Afterparty in the bathroom
☐ Can't move / Never getting out of bed
☐ **Never** drinking again

Where did I wake up?

_____

☐ Alone ☐ With _____ ☐ WTF ☐ Walk of shame

The last thing I remember:

_____
_____

Where I went last night / details:

_____
_____

I drank:

_____
_____
_____

I got:

☐ Buzzed ☐ Wasted
☐ Tipsy ☐ Sh*t-faced
☐ Drunk ☐ Annihilated

I lost:

☐ Keys ☐ Phone ☐ Wallet ☐ Dignity ☐ Other _____

I can't believe I:

☐ Puked—How many times / where / on whom? _____
☐ Drunk dialed / texted / emailed _____
☐ Other awesomeness _____
_____

HOOKUPS

Who: _____ ☐ No clue

Where: _____

Looks: ☆ ☆ ☆ ☆ ☆   ☐ Butt ugly   ☐ Doesn't matter
                                    ☐ Super hot   ☐ Beer goggles

Personality: ☆ ☆ ☆ ☆ ☆   ☐ Zero   ☐ Soul mate
                                            ☐ Just okay   ☐ Who cares

Details: **I think he/she looked like:**

_____

_____

_____

_____

_____

_____

How hot did it get?

☐ ZZZ   ☐ G   ☐ PG   ☐ PG-13   ☐ R   ☐ NC-17   ☐ X   ☐ XXX

Next steps?

☐ Avoid   ☐ Stalk   ☐ Go to church   ☐ Get tested   ☐ Hit that again

Note to self:

_____

_____

Sunglasses are essential for concealing bleary, hungover eyes and making the walk of shame a little less shameful.

HANGOVERS

DATE

Hangover rating ☐ Still drunk

☐ A glass of water and good to go
☐ Greasy breakfast, please
☐ Throbbing headache
☐ Feeling pretty crappy

☐ Everything is spinning
☐ Afterparty in the bathroom
☐ Can't move / Never getting out of bed
☐ **Never** drinking again

Where did I wake up?

_____

☐ Alone ☐ With _____ ☐ WTF ☐ Walk of shame

The last thing I remember:

_____
_____

Where I went last night / details:

_____
_____

I drank:

_____

_____

_____

I got:

☐ Buzzed ☐ Wasted
☐ Tipsy ☐ Sh*t-faced
☐ Drunk ☐ Annihilated

I lost:

☐ Keys ☐ Phone ☐ Wallet ☐ Dignity ☐ Other _____

I can't believe I:

☐ Puked—How many times / where / on whom? _____
☐ Drunk dialed / texted / emailed _____
☐ Other awesomeness _____

HOOKUPS

Who: _____ ☐ No clue

Where: _____

Looks: ☆ ☆ ☆ ☆ ☆   ☐ Butt ugly   ☐ Doesn't matter
                                      ☐ Super hot   ☐ Beer goggles

Personality: ☆ ☆ ☆ ☆ ☆   ☐ Zero   ☐ Soul mate
                                               ☐ Just okay   ☐ Who cares

Details: **I think he/she looked like:**

_____

_____

_____

_____

_____

_____

How hot did it get?

☐ ZZZ   ☐ G   ☐ PG   ☐ PG-13   ☐ R   ☐ NC-17   ☐ X   ☐ XXX

Next steps?

☐ Avoid   ☐ Stalk   ☐ Go to church   ☐ Get tested   ☐ Hit that again

Note to self:

_____

_____

It's been said that drinking a glass of milk or a spoonful of olive oil before consuming alcohol can help prevent a hangover. The milk and oil coat the stomach lining and slow down the absorption of alcohol.

HANGOVERS

DATE

Hangover rating ☐ Still drunk

☐ A glass of water and good to go
☐ Greasy breakfast, please
☐ Throbbing headache
☐ Feeling pretty crappy

☐ Everything is spinning
☐ Afterparty in the bathroom
☐ Can't move / Never getting out of bed
☐ **Never** drinking again

Where did I wake up?

_____

☐ Alone ☐ With _____ ☐ WTF ☐ Walk of shame

The last thing I remember:

_____
_____

Where I went last night / details:

_____
_____

I drank:

_____
_____
_____

I got:

☐ Buzzed ☐ Wasted
☐ Tipsy ☐ Sh*t-faced
☐ Drunk ☐ Annihilated

I lost:

☐ Keys ☐ Phone ☐ Wallet ☐ Dignity ☐ Other _____

I can't believe I:

☐ Puked—How many times / where / on whom? _____
☐ Drunk dialed / texted / emailed _____
☐ Other awesomeness _____

HOOKUPS

Who: _____ ☐ No clue

Where: _____

Looks: ☆ ☆ ☆ ☆ ☆   ☐ Butt ugly   ☐ Doesn't matter
                          ☐ Super hot   ☐ Beer goggles

Personality: ☆ ☆ ☆ ☆ ☆   ☐ Zero   ☐ Soul mate
                                 ☐ Just okay   ☐ Who cares

Details: **I think he/she looked like:**

_____

_____

_____

_____

_____

_____

How hot did it get?

☐ ZZZ   ☐ G   ☐ PG   ☐ PG-13   ☐ R   ☐ NC-17   ☐ X   ☐ XXX

Next steps?

☐ Avoid   ☐ Stalk   ☐ Go to church   ☐ Get tested   ☐ Hit that again

Note to self:

_____

_____

> Remember to drink a glass of water for every glass of alcohol and drink more water before you go to bed. Coconut water is also super hydrating, as it contains essential electrolytes.

HANGOVERS

DATE

Hangover rating ☐ Still drunk

☐ A glass of water and good to go
☐ Greasy breakfast, please
☐ Throbbing headache
☐ Feeling pretty crappy

☐ Everything is spinning
☐ Afterparty in the bathroom
☐ Can't move / Never getting out of bed
☐ **Never** drinking again

Where did I wake up?

_____

☐ Alone ☐ With _____ ☐ WTF ☐ Walk of shame

The last thing I remember:

_____

_____

Where I went last night / details:

_____

_____

I drank:

_____

_____

_____

I got:

☐ Buzzed ☐ Wasted
☐ Tipsy ☐ Sh*t-faced
☐ Drunk ☐ Annihilated

I lost:

☐ Keys ☐ Phone ☐ Wallet ☐ Dignity ☐ Other _____

I can't believe I:

☐ Puked—How many times / where / on whom? _____

☐ Drunk dialed / texted / emailed _____

☐ Other awesomeness _____

HOOKUPS

Who: _____ ☐ No clue

Where: _____

Looks: ☆ ☆ ☆ ☆ ☆   ☐ Butt ugly   ☐ Doesn't matter
                          ☐ Super hot   ☐ Beer goggles

Personality: ☆ ☆ ☆ ☆ ☆   ☐ Zero   ☐ Soul mate
                              ☐ Just okay   ☐ Who cares

Details: **I think he/she looked like:**

_____

_____

_____

_____

_____

_____

How hot did it get?

☐ ZZZ ☐ G ☐ PG ☐ PG-13 ☐ R ☐ NC-17 ☐ X ☐ XXX

Next steps?

☐ Avoid ☐ Stalk ☐ Go to church ☐ Get tested ☐ Hit that again

Note to self:

_____

_____

Consider swapping your bourbon for vodka. Darker liquors contain more
congeners, by-products of alcohol fermentation, which are believed to
make hangovers worse.

HANGOVERS

DATE

Hangover rating ☐ Still drunk

☐ A glass of water and good to go ☐ Everything is spinning
☐ Greasy breakfast, please ☐ Afterparty in the bathroom
☐ Throbbing headache ☐ Can't move / Never getting out of bed
☐ Feeling pretty crappy ☐ **Never** drinking again

Where did I wake up?

_____

☐ Alone ☐ With _____ ☐ WTF ☐ Walk of shame

The last thing I remember:

_____

_____

Where I went last night / details:

_____

_____

I drank:

_____

_____

_____

I got:

☐ Buzzed ☐ Wasted
☐ Tipsy ☐ Sh*t-faced
☐ Drunk ☐ Annihilated

I lost:

☐ Keys ☐ Phone ☐ Wallet ☐ Dignity ☐ Other _____

I can't believe I:

☐ Puked—How many times / where / on whom? _____
☐ Drunk dialed / texted / emailed _____
☐ Other awesomeness _____

HOOKUPS

Who: _____ ☐ No clue

Where: _____

Looks: ☆ ☆ ☆ ☆ ☆   ☐ Butt ugly   ☐ Doesn't matter
                         ☐ Super hot   ☐ Beer goggles

Personality: ☆ ☆ ☆ ☆ ☆   ☐ Zero   ☐ Soul mate
                               ☐ Just okay   ☐ Who cares

Details: **I think he/she looked like:**

_____
_____
_____
_____
_____
_____

How hot did it get?

☐ ZZZ ☐ G ☐ PG ☐ PG-13 ☐ R ☐ NC-17 ☐ X ☐ XXX

Next steps?

☐ Avoid ☐ Stalk ☐ Go to church ☐ Get tested ☐ Hit that again

Note to self:

_____
_____

After a night of fun times, eat something before crawling into bed.
Bananas are a great choice—they contain potassium, which alcohol
consumption depletes from your body, and B_6, which is claimed to
be a great hangover killer.

HANGOVERS

Hangover rating ☐ Still drunk

☐ A glass of water and good to go
☐ Greasy breakfast, please
☐ Throbbing headache
☐ Feeling pretty crappy

☐ Everything is spinning
☐ Afterparty in the bathroom
☐ Can't move / Never getting out of bed
☐ **Never** drinking again

Where did I wake up?

_____

☐ Alone ☐ With _____ ☐ WTF ☐ Walk of shame

The last thing I remember:

_____

_____

Where I went last night / details:

_____

_____

I drank:

_____

_____

_____

I got:

☐ Buzzed ☐ Wasted
☐ Tipsy ☐ Sh*t-faced
☐ Drunk ☐ Annihilated

I lost:

☐ Keys ☐ Phone ☐ Wallet ☐ Dignity ☐ Other _____

I can't believe I:

☐ Puked—How many times / where / on whom? _____
☐ Drunk dialed / texted / emailed _____
☐ Other awesomeness _____

HOOKUPS

Who: _____ ☐ No clue

Where: _____

Looks: ☆ ☆ ☆ ☆ ☆   ☐ Butt ugly   ☐ Doesn't matter
                         ☐ Super hot   ☐ Beer goggles

Personality: ☆ ☆ ☆ ☆ ☆   ☐ Zero   ☐ Soul mate
                              ☐ Just okay   ☐ Who cares

Details: **I think he/she looked like:**

_____

_____

_____

_____

_____

_____

How hot did it get?

☐ ZZZ ☐ G ☐ PG ☐ PG-13 ☐ R ☐ NC-17 ☐ X ☐ XXX

Next steps?

☐ Avoid ☐ Stalk ☐ Go to church ☐ Get tested ☐ Hit that again

Note to self:

_____

_____

If you have friends who think it's funny to write on the passed-out person's forehead, remember to look in a mirror before you leave the house today.

HANGOVERS

DATE

Hangover rating ☐ Still drunk

☐ A glass of water and good to go
☐ Greasy breakfast, please
☐ Throbbing headache
☐ Feeling pretty crappy

☐ Everything is spinning
☐ Afterparty in the bathroom
☐ Can't move / Never getting out of bed
☐ **Never** drinking again

Where did I wake up?

_____

☐ Alone ☐ With _____ ☐ WTF ☐ Walk of shame

The last thing I remember:

_____

_____

Where I went last night / details:

_____

_____

I drank:

_____

_____

_____

I got:

☐ Buzzed ☐ Wasted
☐ Tipsy ☐ Sh*t-faced
☐ Drunk ☐ Annihilated

I lost:

☐ Keys ☐ Phone ☐ Wallet ☐ Dignity ☐ Other _____

I can't believe I:

☐ Puked—How many times / where / on whom? _____
☐ Drunk dialed / texted / emailed _____
☐ Other awesomeness _____

HOOKUPS

Who: _____ ☐ No clue

Where: _____

Looks: ☆ ☆ ☆ ☆ ☆   ☐ Butt ugly   ☐ Doesn't matter
                                 ☐ Super hot   ☐ Beer goggles

Personality: ☆ ☆ ☆ ☆ ☆   ☐ Zero   ☐ Soul mate
                                          ☐ Just okay   ☐ Who cares

Details: **I think he/she looked like:**

_____

_____

_____

_____

_____

_____

How hot did it get?

☐ ZZZ   ☐ G   ☐ PG   ☐ PG-13   ☐ R   ☐ NC-17   ☐ X   ☐ XXX

Next steps?

☐ Avoid   ☐ Stalk   ☐ Go to church   ☐ Get tested   ☐ Hit that again

Note to self:

_____

_____

You're not imagining it: Your hangovers really are getting worse. That's because as you age, you produce less alcohol dehydrogenase, the enzyme that breaks down alcohol.

HANGOVERS

Hangover rating ☐ Still drunk

☐ A glass of water and good to go
☐ Greasy breakfast, please
☐ Throbbing headache
☐ Feeling pretty crappy

☐ Everything is spinning
☐ Afterparty in the bathroom
☐ Can't move / Never getting out of bed
☐ **Never** drinking again

Where did I wake up?

_____

☐ Alone ☐ With _____ ☐ WTF ☐ Walk of shame

The last thing I remember:

_____

_____

Where I went last night / details:

_____

_____

I drank:

_____

_____

_____

I got:

☐ Buzzed   ☐ Wasted
☐ Tipsy   ☐ Sh*t-faced
☐ Drunk   ☐ Annihilated

I lost:

☐ Keys ☐ Phone ☐ Wallet ☐ Dignity ☐ Other _____

I can't believe I:

☐ Puked—How many times / where / on whom? _____
☐ Drunk dialed / texted / emailed _____
☐ Other awesomeness _____

_____

HOOKUPS

Who: _____ ☐ No clue

Where: _____

Looks: ☆ ☆ ☆ ☆ ☆   ☐ Butt ugly   ☐ Doesn't matter
                           ☐ Super hot   ☐ Beer goggles

Personality: ☆ ☆ ☆ ☆ ☆   ☐ Zero   ☐ Soul mate
                                ☐ Just okay   ☐ Who cares

Details: **I think he/she looked like:**

_____
_____
_____
_____
_____
_____

How hot did it get?

☐ ZZZ ☐ G ☐ PG ☐ PG-13 ☐ R ☐ NC-17 ☐ X ☐ XXX

Next steps?

☐ Avoid ☐ Stalk ☐ Go to church ☐ Get tested ☐ Hit that again

Note to self:

_____
_____

Hey, drunky, put down the phone. Drunk dialing or texting always results in embarrassing apology dialing the next day.

HANGOVERS

DATE

Hangover rating ☐ Still drunk

☐ A glass of water and good to go
☐ Greasy breakfast, please
☐ Throbbing headache
☐ Feeling pretty crappy

☐ Everything is spinning
☐ Afterparty in the bathroom
☐ Can't move / Never getting out of bed
☐ **Never** drinking again

Where did I wake up?

_____

☐ Alone ☐ With _____ ☐ WTF ☐ Walk of shame

The last thing I remember:

_____

_____

Where I went last night / details:

_____

_____

I drank:

_____

_____

_____

I got:

☐ Buzzed ☐ Wasted
☐ Tipsy ☐ Sh*t-faced
☐ Drunk ☐ Annihilated

I lost:

☐ Keys ☐ Phone ☐ Wallet ☐ Dignity ☐ Other _____

I can't believe I:

☐ Puked—How many times / where / on whom? _____
☐ Drunk dialed / texted / emailed _____
☐ Other awesomeness _____

HOOKUPS

Who: _____ ☐ No clue

Where: _____

Looks: ☆ ☆ ☆ ☆ ☆   ☐ Butt ugly   ☐ Doesn't matter
                              ☐ Super hot   ☐ Beer goggles

Personality: ☆ ☆ ☆ ☆ ☆   ☐ Zero   ☐ Soul mate
                                   ☐ Just okay   ☐ Who cares

Details: **I think he/she looked like:**

_____

_____

_____

_____

_____

_____

How hot did it get?

☐ ZZZ ☐ G ☐ PG ☐ PG-13 ☐ R ☐ NC-17 ☐ X ☐ XXX

Next steps?

☐ Avoid ☐ Stalk ☐ Go to church ☐ Get tested ☐ Hit that again

Note to self:

_____

_____

Sunglasses are essential for concealing bleary, hungover eyes and making
the walk of shame a little less shameful.

HANGOVERS

DATE

Hangover rating ☐ Still drunk

☐ A glass of water and good to go
☐ Greasy breakfast, please
☐ Throbbing headache
☐ Feeling pretty crappy

☐ Everything is spinning
☐ Afterparty in the bathroom
☐ Can't move / Never getting out of bed
☐ **Never** drinking again

Where did I wake up?

_____

☐ Alone ☐ With _____ ☐ WTF ☐ Walk of shame

The last thing I remember:

_____
_____

Where I went last night / details:

_____
_____

I drank:

_____
_____
_____

I got:

☐ Buzzed ☐ Wasted
☐ Tipsy ☐ Sh*t-faced
☐ Drunk ☐ Annihilated

I lost:

☐ Keys ☐ Phone ☐ Wallet ☐ Dignity ☐ Other _____

I can't believe I:

☐ Puked—How many times / where / on whom? _____
☐ Drunk dialed / texted / emailed _____
☐ Other awesomeness _____

HOOKUPS

Who: _____ ☐ No clue

Where: _____

Looks: ☆ ☆ ☆ ☆ ☆   ☐ Butt ugly   ☐ Doesn't matter
                              ☐ Super hot   ☐ Beer goggles

Personality: ☆ ☆ ☆ ☆ ☆   ☐ Zero   ☐ Soul mate
                                      ☐ Just okay   ☐ Who cares

Details: **I think he/she looked like:**

_____

_____

_____

_____

_____

_____

How hot did it get?

☐ ZZZ   ☐ G   ☐ PG   ☐ PG-13   ☐ R   ☐ NC-17   ☐ X   ☐ XXX

Next steps?

☐ Avoid   ☐ Stalk   ☐ Go to church   ☐ Get tested   ☐ Hit that again

Note to self:

_____

_____

It's been said that drinking a glass of milk or a spoonful of olive oil before consuming alcohol can help prevent a hangover. The milk and oil coat the stomach lining and slow down the absorption of alcohol.

HANGOVERS

Hangover rating ☐ Still drunk

☐ A glass of water and good to go
☐ Greasy breakfast, please
☐ Throbbing headache
☐ Feeling pretty crappy

☐ Everything is spinning
☐ Afterparty in the bathroom
☐ Can't move / Never getting out of bed
☐ **Never** drinking again

Where did I wake up?

_____

☐ Alone ☐ With _____ ☐ WTF ☐ Walk of shame

The last thing I remember:

_____
_____

Where I went last night / details:

_____
_____

I drank:

_____

_____

_____

I got:

☐ Buzzed ☐ Wasted
☐ Tipsy ☐ Sh*t-faced
☐ Drunk ☐ Annihilated

I lost:

☐ Keys ☐ Phone ☐ Wallet ☐ Dignity ☐ Other _____

I can't believe I:

☐ Puked—How many times / where / on whom? _____
☐ Drunk dialed / texted / emailed _____
☐ Other awesomeness _____

HOOKUPS

Who: _____ ☐ No clue

Where: _____

Looks: ☆ ☆ ☆ ☆ ☆   ☐ Butt ugly   ☐ Doesn't matter
                               ☐ Super hot   ☐ Beer goggles

Personality: ☆ ☆ ☆ ☆ ☆   ☐ Zero   ☐ Soul mate
                                  ☐ Just okay   ☐ Who cares

Details: **I think he/she looked like:**

_____

_____

_____

_____

_____

_____

How hot did it get?

☐ ZZZ   ☐ G   ☐ PG   ☐ PG-13   ☐ R   ☐ NC-17   ☐ X   ☐ XXX

Next steps?

☐ Avoid   ☐ Stalk   ☐ Go to church   ☐ Get tested   ☐ Hit that again

Note to self:

_____

_____

> Remember to drink a glass of water for every glass of alcohol and drink
> more water before you go to bed. Coconut water is also super hydrating,
> as it contains essential electrolytes.

HANGOVERS

Hangover rating ☐ Still drunk

☐ A glass of water and good to go
☐ Greasy breakfast, please
☐ Throbbing headache
☐ Feeling pretty crappy

☐ Everything is spinning
☐ Afterparty in the bathroom
☐ Can't move / Never getting out of bed
☐ **Never** drinking again

Where did I wake up?

_____

☐ Alone ☐ With _____ ☐ WTF ☐ Walk of shame

The last thing I remember:

_____

_____

Where I went last night / details:

_____

_____

I drank:

_____

_____

_____

I got:

☐ Buzzed ☐ Wasted
☐ Tipsy ☐ Sh*t-faced
☐ Drunk ☐ Annihilated

I lost:

☐ Keys ☐ Phone ☐ Wallet ☐ Dignity ☐ Other _____

I can't believe I:

☐ Puked—How many times / where / on whom? _____

☐ Drunk dialed / texted / emailed _____

☐ Other awesomeness _____

_____

HOOKUPS

Who: _____ ☐ No clue

Where: _____

Looks: ☆ ☆ ☆ ☆ ☆   ☐ Butt ugly   ☐ Doesn't matter
                          ☐ Super hot   ☐ Beer goggles

Personality: ☆ ☆ ☆ ☆ ☆   ☐ Zero   ☐ Soul mate
                                ☐ Just okay ☐ Who cares

Details: **I think he/she looked like:**

_____

_____

_____

_____

_____

_____

How hot did it get?

☐ ZZZ ☐ G ☐ PG ☐ PG-13 ☐ R ☐ NC-17 ☐ X ☐ XXX

Next steps?

☐ Avoid ☐ Stalk ☐ Go to church ☐ Get tested ☐ Hit that again

Note to self:

_____

_____

Consider swapping your bourbon for vodka. Darker liquors contain more congeners, by-products of alcohol fermentation, which are believed to make hangovers worse.

HANGOVERS

DATE

Hangover rating ☐ Still drunk

☐ A glass of water and good to go
☐ Greasy breakfast, please
☐ Throbbing headache
☐ Feeling pretty crappy

☐ Everything is spinning
☐ Afterparty in the bathroom
☐ Can't move / Never getting out of bed
☐ **Never** drinking again

Where did I wake up?

_____

☐ Alone ☐ With _____ ☐ WTF ☐ Walk of shame

The last thing I remember:

_____

_____

Where I went last night / details:

_____

_____

I drank:

_____

_____

_____

I got:

☐ Buzzed ☐ Wasted
☐ Tipsy ☐ Sh*t-faced
☐ Drunk ☐ Annihilated

I lost:

☐ Keys ☐ Phone ☐ Wallet ☐ Dignity ☐ Other _____

I can't believe I:

☐ Puked—How many times / where / on whom? _____
☐ Drunk dialed / texted / emailed _____
☐ Other awesomeness _____

_____

HOOKUPS

Who: _____ ☐ No clue

Where: _____

Looks: ☆ ☆ ☆ ☆ ☆   ☐ Butt ugly   ☐ Doesn't matter
                                 ☐ Super hot   ☐ Beer goggles

Personality: ☆ ☆ ☆ ☆ ☆   ☐ Zero   ☐ Soul mate
                                        ☐ Just okay   ☐ Who cares

Details: **I think he/she looked like:**

_____

_____

_____

_____

_____

_____

How hot did it get?

☐ ZZZ   ☐ G   ☐ PG   ☐ PG-13   ☐ R   ☐ NC-17   ☐ X   ☐ XXX

Next steps?

☐ Avoid   ☐ Stalk   ☐ Go to church   ☐ Get tested   ☐ Hit that again

Note to self:

_____

_____

After a night of fun times, eat something before crawling into bed.
Bananas are a great choice—they contain potassium, which alcohol
consumption depletes from your body, and B_6, which is claimed to
be a great hangover killer.

HANGOVERS

DATE

Hangover rating ☐ Still drunk

☐ A glass of water and good to go
☐ Greasy breakfast, please
☐ Throbbing headache
☐ Feeling pretty crappy

☐ Everything is spinning
☐ Afterparty in the bathroom
☐ Can't move / Never getting out of bed
☐ **Never** drinking again

Where did I wake up?

_____

☐ Alone ☐ With _____ ☐ WTF ☐ Walk of shame

The last thing I remember:

_____

_____

Where I went last night / details:

_____

_____

I drank:

_____

_____

_____

I got:

☐ Buzzed   ☐ Wasted
☐ Tipsy   ☐ Sh*t-faced
☐ Drunk   ☐ Annihilated

I lost:

☐ Keys ☐ Phone ☐ Wallet ☐ Dignity ☐ Other _____

I can't believe I:

☐ Puked—How many times / where / on whom? _____

☐ Drunk dialed / texted / emailed _____

☐ Other awesomeness _____

HOOKUPS

Who: _____ ☐ No clue

Where: _____

Looks: ☆ ☆ ☆ ☆ ☆   ☐ Butt ugly   ☐ Doesn't matter
                                    ☐ Super hot   ☐ Beer goggles

Personality: ☆ ☆ ☆ ☆ ☆   ☐ Zero   ☐ Soul mate
                                           ☐ Just okay   ☐ Who cares

Details: **I think he/she looked like:**

_____

_____

_____

_____

_____

_____

How hot did it get?

☐ ZZZ ☐ G ☐ PG ☐ PG-13 ☐ R ☐ NC-17 ☐ X ☐ XXX

Next steps?

☐ Avoid ☐ Stalk ☐ Go to church ☐ Get tested ☐ Hit that again

Note to self:

_____

_____

If you have friends who think it's funny to write on the passed-out
person's forehead, remember to look in a mirror before you leave the
house today.

HANGOVERS

DATE

Hangover rating ☐ Still drunk

☐ A glass of water and good to go
☐ Greasy breakfast, please
☐ Throbbing headache
☐ Feeling pretty crappy

☐ Everything is spinning
☐ Afterparty in the bathroom
☐ Can't move / Never getting out of bed
☐ **Never** drinking again

Where did I wake up?

_____

☐ Alone ☐ With _____ ☐ WTF ☐ Walk of shame

The last thing I remember:

_____

_____

Where I went last night / details:

_____

_____

I drank:

_____

_____

_____

I got:

☐ Buzzed ☐ Wasted
☐ Tipsy ☐ Sh*t-faced
☐ Drunk ☐ Annihilated

I lost:

☐ Keys ☐ Phone ☐ Wallet ☐ Dignity ☐ Other _____

I can't believe I:

☐ Puked—How many times / where / on whom? _____

☐ Drunk dialed / texted / emailed _____

☐ Other awesomeness _____

_____

HOOKUPS

Who: _____ ☐ No clue

Where: _____

Looks: ☆ ☆ ☆ ☆ ☆   ☐ Butt ugly   ☐ Doesn't matter
                              ☐ Super hot   ☐ Beer goggles

Personality: ☆ ☆ ☆ ☆ ☆   ☐ Zero   ☐ Soul mate
                                     ☐ Just okay   ☐ Who cares

Details: **I think he/she looked like:**

_____

_____

_____

_____

_____

_____

How hot did it get?

☐ ZZZ   ☐ G   ☐ PG   ☐ PG-13   ☐ R   ☐ NC-17   ☐ X   ☐ XXX

Next steps?

☐ Avoid   ☐ Stalk   ☐ Go to church   ☐ Get tested   ☐ Hit that again

Note to self:

_____

_____

> You're not imagining it: Your hangovers really are getting worse. That's because as you age, you produce less alcohol dehydrogenase, the enzyme that breaks down alcohol.

HANGOVERS

DATE

Hangover rating   ☐ Still drunk

☐ A glass of water and good to go
☐ Greasy breakfast, please
☐ Throbbing headache
☐ Feeling pretty crappy

☐ Everything is spinning
☐ Afterparty in the bathroom
☐ Can't move / Never getting out of bed
☐ **Never** drinking again

Where did I wake up?

_____

☐ Alone ☐ With _____ ☐ WTF ☐ Walk of shame

The last thing I remember:

_____

_____

Where I went last night / details:

_____

_____

I drank:

_____

_____

_____

I got:

☐ Buzzed ☐ Wasted
☐ Tipsy ☐ Sh*t-faced
☐ Drunk ☐ Annihilated

I lost:

☐ Keys ☐ Phone ☐ Wallet ☐ Dignity ☐ Other _____

I can't believe I:

☐ Puked—How many times / where / on whom? _____

☐ Drunk dialed / texted / emailed _____

☐ Other awesomeness _____

_____

HOOKUPS

Who: _____ ☐ No clue

Where: _____

Looks: ☆ ☆ ☆ ☆ ☆   ☐ Butt ugly   ☐ Doesn't matter
                             ☐ Super hot   ☐ Beer goggles

Personality: ☆ ☆ ☆ ☆ ☆   ☐ Zero   ☐ Soul mate
                                       ☐ Just okay   ☐ Who cares

Details: **I think he/she looked like:**

_____

_____

_____

_____

_____

_____

How hot did it get?
☐ ZZZ ☐ G ☐ PG ☐ PG-13 ☐ R ☐ NC-17 ☐ X ☐ XXX

Next steps?
☐ Avoid ☐ Stalk ☐ Go to church ☐ Get tested ☐ Hit that again

Note to self:

_____

_____

> Hey, drunky, put down the phone. Drunk dialing or texting always results in embarrassing apology dialing the next day.

HANGOVERS

Hangover rating ☐ Still drunk

☐ A glass of water and good to go

☐ Greasy breakfast, please

☐ Throbbing headache

☐ Feeling pretty crappy

☐ Everything is spinning

☐ Afterparty in the bathroom

☐ Can't move / Never getting out of bed

☐ **Never** drinking again

Where did I wake up?

_____

☐ Alone ☐ With _____ ☐ WTF ☐ Walk of shame

The last thing I remember:

_____

_____

Where I went last night / details:

_____

_____

I drank:

_____

_____

_____

I got:

☐ Buzzed ☐ Wasted

☐ Tipsy ☐ Sh*t-faced

☐ Drunk ☐ Annihilated

I lost:

☐ Keys ☐ Phone ☐ Wallet ☐ Dignity ☐ Other _____

I can't believe I:

☐ Puked—How many times / where / on whom? _____

☐ Drunk dialed / texted / emailed _____

☐ Other awesomeness _____

_____

HOOKUPS

Who: _____ ☐ No clue

Where: _____

Looks: ☆ ☆ ☆ ☆ ☆   ☐ Butt ugly   ☐ Doesn't matter
                                   ☐ Super hot   ☐ Beer goggles

Personality: ☆ ☆ ☆ ☆ ☆   ☐ Zero   ☐ Soul mate
                                           ☐ Just okay   ☐ Who cares

Details: **I think he/she looked like:**

_____

_____

_____

_____

_____

_____

How hot did it get?

☐ ZZZ   ☐ G   ☐ PG   ☐ PG-13   ☐ R   ☐ NC-17   ☐ X   ☐ XXX

Next steps?

☐ Avoid   ☐ Stalk   ☐ Go to church   ☐ Get tested   ☐ Hit that again

Note to self:

_____

_____

Sunglasses are essential for concealing bleary, hungover eyes and making
the walk of shame a little less shameful.

HANGOVERS

DATE

Hangover rating ☐ Still drunk

☐ A glass of water and good to go
☐ Greasy breakfast, please
☐ Throbbing headache
☐ Feeling pretty crappy

☐ Everything is spinning
☐ Afterparty in the bathroom
☐ Can't move / Never getting out of bed
☐ **Never** drinking again

Where did I wake up?

_____

☐ Alone ☐ With _____ ☐ WTF ☐ Walk of shame

The last thing I remember:

_____

_____

Where I went last night / details:

_____

_____

I drank:

_____

_____

_____

I got:

☐ Buzzed ☐ Wasted
☐ Tipsy ☐ Sh*t-faced
☐ Drunk ☐ Annihilated

I lost:

☐ Keys ☐ Phone ☐ Wallet ☐ Dignity ☐ Other _____

I can't believe I:

☐ Puked—How many times / where / on whom? _____

☐ Drunk dialed / texted / emailed _____

☐ Other awesomeness _____

_____

HOOKUPS

Who: _____ ☐ No clue

Where: _____

Looks: ☆ ☆ ☆ ☆ ☆   ☐ Butt ugly   ☐ Doesn't matter
                          ☐ Super hot   ☐ Beer goggles

Personality: ☆ ☆ ☆ ☆ ☆   ☐ Zero   ☐ Soul mate
                                ☐ Just okay   ☐ Who cares

Details: **I think he/she looked like:**

_____

_____

_____

_____

_____

_____

How hot did it get?

☐ ZZZ ☐ G ☐ PG ☐ PG-13 ☐ R ☐ NC-17 ☐ X ☐ XXX

Next steps?

☐ Avoid ☐ Stalk ☐ Go to church ☐ Get tested ☐ Hit that again

Note to self:

_____

_____

It's been said that drinking a glass of milk or a spoonful of olive oil before consuming alcohol can help prevent a hangover. The milk and oil coat the stomach lining and slow down the absorption of alcohol.

HANGOVERS

DATE

Hangover rating ☐ Still drunk

☐ A glass of water and good to go
☐ Greasy breakfast, please
☐ Throbbing headache
☐ Feeling pretty crappy

☐ Everything is spinning
☐ Afterparty in the bathroom
☐ Can't move / Never getting out of bed
☐ **Never** drinking again

Where did I wake up?

_____

☐ Alone ☐ With _____ ☐ WTF ☐ Walk of shame

The last thing I remember:

_____
_____

Where I went last night / details:

_____
_____

I drank:

_____
_____
_____

I got:

☐ Buzzed ☐ Wasted
☐ Tipsy ☐ Sh*t-faced
☐ Drunk ☐ Annihilated

I lost:

☐ Keys ☐ Phone ☐ Wallet ☐ Dignity ☐ Other _____

I can't believe I:

☐ Puked—How many times / where / on whom? _____
☐ Drunk dialed / texted / emailed _____
☐ Other awesomeness _____
_____

HOOKUPS

Who: _____ ☐ No clue

Where: _____

Looks: ☆ ☆ ☆ ☆ ☆   ☐ Butt ugly   ☐ Doesn't matter
                                ☐ Super hot   ☐ Beer goggles

Personality: ☆ ☆ ☆ ☆ ☆   ☐ Zero   ☐ Soul mate
                                       ☐ Just okay   ☐ Who cares

Details: **I think he/she looked like:**

_____

_____

_____

_____

_____

_____

How hot did it get?

☐ ZZZ   ☐ G   ☐ PG   ☐ PG-13   ☐ R   ☐ NC-17   ☐ X   ☐ XXX

Next steps?

☐ Avoid   ☐ Stalk   ☐ Go to church   ☐ Get tested   ☐ Hit that again

Note to self:

_____

_____

> Remember to drink a glass of water for every glass of alcohol and drink
> more water before you go to bed. Coconut water is also super hydrating,
> as it contains essential electrolytes.